Dropshipping and Ecommerce

Build A $20,000 per Month Business by Making Money Online with Shopify, Amazon FBA, Affiliate Marketing, Facebook Advertising and eBay Selling (+50 Passive Income Ideas)

Max Plitt

consent and can in no way be considered an endorsement from the trademark holder.

Table of Contents

Introduction

Online business or e-business refers to any kind of entrepreneurial activity that occurs over the internet. Operating such a business includes the provision of services or buying and selling of different products. A business owner who conducts all or part of their business online is said to be operating an online business.

Anyone can start and run their online business. All you need is a great product, a unique idea or even just a trending product. If you have any of these, then you can easily begin selling online. It is a process that is very similar to ordinary trading, except that, this time, your shop is online.

Online Businesses Are Scalable

Almost all online business models are scalable and building a scalable business is one of the factors that you should consider. This means that it is okay to start small and then scale up to whatever size you desire.

A scalable business is simply any business that has the ability to cope and thrive under increased demand for its products or services. For instance, if you are a personal trainer, then you are limited by how many clients you can take on. Time limits you because you can only work for so many hours each day.

On the contrary, if you sell products or digital products such as online training and meal plans, then you can easily scale up as the demand grows. To scale up successfully, you need to come up with a great product, leverage automation, and software, create procedures and templates, outsource some tasks to others and generally provide excellent customer service.

According to experts, online businesses fit the scalable business model best. A huge number of consumers prefer to shop online from the comfort of their homes using their phones or other devices. Building a successful and scalable business calls for the ability to grow without the need to spend excessively or trade more time for money. Some of the best, yet scalable, online businesses include affiliate marketing, dropshipping, online stores and so on.

Learn to Build Confidence and Overcome Obstacles

It is easy to feel discouraged when you start an online business. It can seem like a daunting task. Fortunately, it is possible to build up your confidence and overcome any obstacles that you may encounter. Remember that you need to have a thick skin if you are to successfully build an online business.

You need to affirm yourself, then visualize where you want to go. Affirmations are a powerful tool deliberately designed to instill positive beliefs about you. And remember that what the mind can conceive and believe in, the heart can actually achieve. You have probably been criticizing yourself for a long time, but the outcome has never been positive. You should, instead, try and approve yourself and see how it goes. Finally, learn how to take rejection. Most business owners encounter instances of rejection regularly. These can have a negative effect on you if not handled well. Learn how to handle rejections and then simply set yourself up to win.

You Have Sufficient Time for A Side Hustle (Even If Working Elsewhere)

Having a side-hustle while working at another job can be very lucrative. It is absolutely possible to start and run your own online business even if you are employed. The most crucial process that will determine your success is planning. You need to create a list of all the things you need to do and then prioritize them. If there are certain things that you have to do, you should put these down on a list and think about when you can find the time.

Check out your diary and calendar and find times when you'd normally be free. If there are free moments here and there, plan how to use these moments to work on your business. Identifying strategic activities that need to be done right away is absolutely crucial for your success. Remembering that the hours you put in add up is key. 1 hour each day is easily achievable making that 7 hours a week where you're investing time into your business to reach success closer and closer each day.

Five Common Mistakes That People Make When Starting an Online Business

Starting an online business is never easy. There are challenges along the way. Fortunately, most of these challenges can be overcome. An online business can also be an exciting time in your life. You get to own a business, earn money and gain financial freedom. However, you really need to watch out for some mistakes that can pull you down.

One of the top mistakes that online business owners make is starting a business without a plan. A business plan is not just essential, but vital if you are to succeed. It empowers you to understand what you need to know in order to serve your clients. When you are able to understand what your target audience needs, then you will be able to meet the appropriate demands, identify the products or services they need and market to them.

Sometimes, an entrepreneur will come up with a poor-quality website or a webhost that is unreliable. On the internet, time is money, so if your clients cannot access your website, you will lose money. Remember that customers shop regularly, be it day or night. As such, you need to ensure that your website is functional and accessible at all times. To do this, you need an absolutely reliable webhost, as well as a professionally-designed website.

Sometimes, entrepreneurs fail to provide appropriate customer service. Customer service is absolutely important and you should excel in it. While you may not see your customers face to face, it is still crucial that you provide excellent service to them. This means answering their phone queries, responding to their emails, and processing their orders instantaneously. Remember that your store's success largely depends on your reputation and trust; therefore, step up your customer service efforts and you will thrive.

Failure can happen when we do not gather information or research to find out about other competitors stores in the same niche. Studying the playing field is important. There are many reasons for this, including pricing, in-demand products, trends, finding what they are doing well and not so well in etc. Also, do not fret so much about costs and expenses. While it is normal to want to save as much as possible, you should not cut back your expenditure that it affects the quality of the significant elements of your business such as logo, website and your business name.

Research your competitors thoroughly and one up them in everything they do!

Active Income versus Passive Income

If you have a job where you work most of the day and earn a salary, this can be referred to as your active source of income, because you are actively engaged in actual revenue-generating activities.

On the other hand, we have what is known as a passive income. This is income that you generate as you engage in other activities. People have been known to generate income from investments such as Dropshipping, affiliate marketing, Facebook ads, eBay selling, Amazon FBA and MANY other possible sources while sleeping, playing golf, studying.

Passive income means Freedom. You do what you want when you want.

This is the beauty of online business and if you have your own online business, you will be earning a passive income. This means that you will be making money as you sleep, eat and do all other things that you love. An online e-commerce business is an ideal income-generating venture. People will visit your website and buy products or pay for services and thereby generate you a profit even when you are away. Of course, you still have to do some occasional work, once you get things running but you will mostly be earning a passive income with your store.

Now a mistake people make is falling for this Passive lifestyle. Yes online business is very passive and you can make it passive quite easily. However this does not mean that you don't have to put in the hard work when starting out. You need to put this before anything else if you want to achieve freedom so do not get caught up in this and think that you can just relax and do a little work here and there when starting out.

Invest More to Receive More

When you start your first online business, you will most likely not have all the finances that you need. As such, you should try and save as much as possible. Nevertheless, if you wish to make more money, then, you will probably have to spend a lot more. Your business is not going to grow itself. You will need to put in a lot of time and effort. In addition, you will probably need to make a financial investment to get a good return.

Some of the tasks that will require either your time or money include the following:

- Social media and marketing
- Bookkeeping
- Administrative tasks
- Product packaging
- Graphic design
- Website and web design
- Product photography

- Shipment and fulfillment
- Production of goods
- Creating and managing wholesale relationships

At the onset, you will be focusing on all these things. You will probably have more money than time in your hands. With the passage of time, you will start getting more customers and sales. If this happens, you will need to increase your inventory or pay more for additional costs and charges depending on the market's demand.

As you get more customers, you will be required to invest more time processing orders and processing payments. You may not have thought about this, but investing your profits back into your business might just be necessary. By doing so, you will be investing in the future growth of your business. Plenty of successful business owners testify to re-investing profits back into their businesses if you don't do this you will fall behind, stay at the same income or even worse start all over again.

A successful business is one that is well-managed and also well-funded.

Chapter 1: Basics of Online Business

E-commerce can be described as the art of providing services or selling products over the internet. This is as opposed to ordinary stores, shops, and outlets that are located in physical establishments. Online trading has redefined the modern marketplace. There are more and more people starting up their own businesses and selling online, but even more who are choosing to buy through mobile devices like smartphones.

When you think about starting your own online business, you could be excited at the prospect of being your own boss, at the expected freedom as well as the financial freedom expected to come your way. This kind of excitement is common. Even then, there are those who are apprehensive. They doubt themselves and are unsure about their own discipline and productivity. The fear of becoming unproductive or being lazy keeps some from venturing into the online business space. The key is setting mini goals and setting a to-do list to over come every obstacle that stands in your way.

Running An Online Business

Just like many other new ideas, online trading has its own ups and down. There are advantages and disadvantages of running your own business over the internet. Before venturing into business, you should learn about some of these pros and cons. These cons are not something that you should be scared of, these are just to increase your awareness and know exactly what you're up for so you can stay prepared and on point everyday.

As a prospective business owner, it is imperative that you look beyond all the hype and focus on developing your own perspective on the real value of online business. This is because there are plenty of benefits of this mode of business, but most are targeted towards customers. However, they can sometimes be unfavorable to businesses and traders.

Elimination of geographical borders: One of the most significant benefits of having an online business is that geographical limitations are largely eliminated. When you own a store-based business, your customer base is usually limited to local consumers. This is because customers have to physically visit your store. However, when your business is online, then anyone can buy from your store. This greatly enhances your chances of reach, increasing profitability and success.

Advantages of online businesses

Feeling of achievement: When you start your own business, one of the things that happen is that you gain a sense of responsibility that jolts you out of your comfort zone. You also get to realize the kind of useful service that you are providing to your customers and feel a great sense of satisfaction. It is a great feeling to own and manage a business that serves others. You will feel the urge to work even harder and put in more effort in order to run and grow a profitable business.

Start on a tiny budget: Unlike brick and mortar stores that require hundreds or thousands of dollars to set up, online businesses are relatively easy to start. You are not required to build an inventory, costly overheads, or pay for rental space. All you need is a website, a computer, and access to the internet. With these at hand, you can begin your own online business. Think about a blog, for instance, you can easily launch your own blog at zero upfront costs if you make use of websites like WordPress or Blogger.

Gain access to the global market: Online business opens doors to global trading. This will largely depend on the kind of niche that you choose. If you are selling small fashion items, for instance, you can sell to clients located virtually around the world.

Numerous payment options: You also gain access to numerous payment methods. Just about all online trading platforms can accept and process payments made using credit cards, PayPal, Stripe, and others. These payment options can be used by both global clients and local customers. The kind of security available today keeps everyone safe.

Affordable marketing options to attract customers: Regular brick and mortar businesses spend a ton of cash advertising their brands, products, and services. This money is often spent on expensive marketing campaigns including advertisements on TV and radio, posters, flyers, etc. While these are costly, returns are never guaranteed. Fortunately, online trading makes use of very effective yet relatively low-cost options, such as SEO marketing, PPC, pay per impression and others.

Save money on costs: Since your business functions online, you are able to save on different costs including rent, overheads, the need for inventory and so much more. Physical stores are expensive to sustain while online businesses lack the need for most costs especially rent and overheads.

It is also beneficial to you when you grow because sometimes growth can be virtually unlimited. It is possible to sell as much stock as you can if you adopt the e-commerce model. This way, the store can remain open all day and all night. Consumers will be able to view your products at any time of the day or night.

Ability to sell digital goods: Apart from physical goods that you sell through your store, customers can also purchase digital goods such as books, albums, music, videos, courses, training and so on. This is not just convenient but also saves you the hassle of having to mail goods to customers.

Scaling up: An online business is easier to scale-up compared to regular business. This is because it lacks the limitations visibly present on brick and mortar enterprises. They are not bound by any physical limitations such as store size, finances and so on. It is also pretty easy to link up the entire supply chain to a business-to-business e-commerce system. This makes the entire process transparent, easy to execute, cheaper, and fast. Also, you will not need to handle any cash, so this will help cut down on costs and eliminate possible accounting errors.

Track logistics: And finally, an online business makes it easy to track your packages and this is an ideal situation for any successful business. When you or your customers are able to track packages in real time, then you can have an idea of how far it is before eventual receipt.

What You Have To Look Out For In Online Business

Duplication: It is very easy for someone else to copy and implement your idea. There are hundreds of others out there seeking to identify profitable online businesses and imitate them. Cloning, duplication, and copying of successful ideas are common and will cause you to lower your prices and become less profitable.

Disadvantages over brick and mortar stores: There are a couple of cons of an online business compared to brick and mortar establishments. There are still plenty of customers who prefer visiting local stores and malls. They love the personal touch and the shopping experience which can be lacking online. Also, there are customers who prefer to experience a product before actually buying it. These reasons are a genuine con of online stores compared to regular stores.

These are sufficient reasons to instill fear in customers because they may not be able to identify scams. As an online trader, you have to make sure that your website is secure and has the necessary security features that protect against fraud, phishing, theft, and all other risks. Also building trust and a relationship with your customer online is something that will generate more sales within your online store

Lack of instant gratification: If shopping is all about instant gratification, then online stores would be unable to provide that. Customers who visit regular brick and mortar stores get to purchase items and enjoy instant possession of their purchases.

On the contrary, online shoppers have to wait days and sometimes weeks to receive their purchases. If not, then they may be forced to pay for premium shipping. Additionally, customers who do not like their purchases usually return them and the business is forced to issue a refund. Reverse logistics functions where a customer has to send back their purchase can be expensive and disheartening. There is also a myriad of taxes that you may be subjected to. When you open an online business, regulators or government authorities may require you to be registered, pay for a license and also pay taxes regularly. Tax regimes are not clearly defined when it comes to transactions within different regions. All these hurdles can hold you back from starting an online business.

Factors that favor customers but bad for businesses: There are a couple of factors that do not favor businesses but are great for consumers. Take for instance price comparisons. Customers are able to compare prices across different stores in order to find stores selling the most affordable products. Sadly, traders are quite able to compare the prices at competing stores. Such websites are restricted as business revenues sometimes get omitted from searches.

Customers also enjoy numerous discounts, promos, sales, and lots of other campaigns that see lower prices and other benefits. However, there are no corresponding benefits to sellers. These discounts are often meant to gain an upper hand against competitors. Consumers also enjoy the convenience of goods delivered to their addresses, but the complexity of the process is often partly borne by the sellers.

Training and patience: In some instances, you will need some training and patience before profits start coming your way. Most of the training efforts should go towards marketing and quality customer service.

Self-realization: Since you will have no boss, chances of slacking and procrastination can be pretty high. You are likely to neglect some work or postpone some chores and so on. This is why self-realization and punctuality are so important. You will really need to become self-disciplined and dedicate yourself to your business.

Emotions: It is possible to go through a myriad of emotions as you trade online. A lot of people start off hoping to make profits right away. This is unlikely to happen because of numerous reasons. However, remember that success comes after a few failures. If you can keep your emotions in check, then you will soon be smiling all the way to the bank.

It is important to point out that a passive income will not materialize right away, but will most likely take a while. Before your business becomes self-sustaining, you will need to put in all the hard work, the time, effort, and resources. You may have to pump any profits back into the business, write blogs, engage with your customers and so much more. However, eventually, your business will thrive and will become self-sustaining.

A day in the life of an online trader

I wake up in the morning at about 9:00am, (yeah that's late but that's the beauty of making money online) I then prepare myself, and check my phone. At this time of the day, I am likely to find plenty of messages from my customers, partners, and associates. These could be emails, chats, and general messages on my website. I try to respond to as many of these messages as possible. It is crucial that the business keeps running without any hindrances so I make a point of clearing up any pending quests and things like that. I also check out my social media sites and see what people are saying. I try and respond to as many messages on social media and engage with clients or customers.

By midmorning, I am seated on my workstation and start doing some real work. The work involves liaising with shippers and suppliers. Later in the day, I'll probably sit down and write my blog. After that, I have the rest of the day free. You notice that I only put in real work for only about three to four hours each day. This frees me up to focus on other things that I love and enjoy doing.

Therefore, as a successful online business owner, you will spend only a couple of hours each day working and handling work-related matters. For the rest of the day, you will be free to engage in activities that you actually enjoy doing. For instance, you can take a walk to the beach, go shopping, or watch your favorite TV shows. There are plenty of people living their dream lives. You, too, can live your best life if you can successfully set up your own online business.

Preferred Niche – Photography

As a trader, I prefer selling professional cameras and accessories. There is a reason for this choice. The first is that there is a market out there for individuals seeking good quality cameras. Amateur and professional photographers love to use good quality cameras for their work. Take bloggers and traders for instance. They desire large, good quality, colorful and clear images for their work. All these individuals will search for the best quality cameras and they will come across my website.

As a trader and online business owner, I first do my research on Amazon and other platforms to find the latest and best quality cameras. I want to find their specifics and out how much they cost. I will then find images of these photos and some literature about them. I then ensure that my website is very presentable so that all customers would be interested buy from me. However, I do not stock even a single camera. I instead automate my website so that any purchases are directed to Amazon website which then processes the orders while I receive a share of the profits.

Preferred niche – photography: Another reason why I prefer this niche is that there is zero likelihood of returns. When you operate in sectors such as fashion, you will likely to receive a lot of returns. This is not good for business because it will cost you, annoy your shippers, and dishearten you.

On the other hand, quality gadgets targeted at a niche customer base will hardly be returned. Customers know what they need and they trust the brands. They will receive good quality products from reputable companies and therefore chances of returns are minimal.

Profits: It is possible to make serious profits when you sell expensive items. The average camera costs between $300 and several thousand dollars. If you add even a markup of $200 - $500 per item, you will make a neat profit and there will be almost zero costs to you. As a result, you will make big money and become profitable within a reasonable period of time.

Suppose you only sell 10 items each day and earn a profit of $200 each time. This adds up to a profit of $200 * 10 = $2,000 each day. If you can repeat this every day, you will then make $60,000 per month and $720,000 each year. Nowhere else will you make this kind of money except by selling at your own online store.

If you notice the criteria used in selecting the product to sell, you will see that we chose a specific niche such as professional photography. You should avoid general niches such as men's fashion, women's clothing, and so on. While the general population provides a large market, you will fare much better with a smaller but more determined niche market.

Also, notice that we chose a product with very little chances of returns. Fashion items are very notorious for returns. Returns can be expensive and disheartening. Avoid products that can easily be returned. Finally, identify costly products that allow you to factor in a decent profit. If you sell products worth $20 or less, you will make very little money and will be forced to sell hundreds of units each day to be profitable.

Shiny Object Syndrome (SOS)

There is a phenomenon that is affecting business owners. It appears to be a trend but is not a positive one. Online entrepreneurs can get distracted by numerous other business ideas. This is called Shiny Object Syndrome. Now, the importance of picking one business idea and sticking to that at the start is crucial. Don't get caught up in other peoples success or the lack of success in your business source.

When a business owner sees a new idea, they can get so obsessed with it that they get distracted from their current business. This is typical of the SOS.

This phenomenon does not just affect small business owners. It affects all business owners and managers, including leaders of large conglomerates and corporations. However, you should ask yourself some significant questions before embarking on a new business. Is it really right for you? Do you need to spend time pursuing yet another business venture? Will you be able to complete this new venture as required or will it simply be a waste of time, energy, and resources?

Basically, it is okay to pursue other business interests. However, it is advisable to stick to one business idea and give it your best in order to become profitable and thrive.

Chapter 2: Create Success through Dropshipping

What is Dropshipping?

Dropshipping is a business model that allows a business to sell a product it does not manufacture and with no inventory at all. Any orders that such a business receives are processed at a fulfillment center. The business will not handle or even see the products but will receive their share of the profits and deal with any customer service.

In such a model, online business owners will partner with a fulfillment warehouse that will process and ship all incoming orders. The most prominent play on the Shopify platform is Oberlo. Oberlo is the most important partner on Shopify and makes use of AliExpress.

We can breakdown dropshipping into three main components. These are:

- A customer places an order on my online store
- The order is forwarded to my dropshipping partner
- The partner then processes the order and ships the item to my customer

The Pros and Cons of Dropshipping

A lot of people start dropshipping business believing it is an easy venture to operate. They believe that since there is no need for inventory, then they can expect no problems. However, this is far from true.

The truth is that nothing is ever easy. Each solution has its own set of problems. However, if you can overcome some of these challenges, you will then be set to enjoy success and profitability.

The pros or advantages of dropshipping

1. Low Startup Costs: Starting up a dropshipping business requires relatively low capital. For starters, you do not need to invest in any stock or inventory items. All you need is a website from platforms such as Shopify, a niche, your own computer and access to the internet.

The low-cost nature of dropshipping has made it an ideal business for entrepreneurs with little or no income. All you need to do is to identify a suitable dropshipping partner and immediately begin making money. This model has worked for numerous traders around the world and will also work for you.

2. Low inventory cost: As discussed earlier, you do not need to invest any capital into buying inventory items. This is not necessary. Most other types of businesses are usually crippled by the large capital requirements for inventory items. Therefore, with almost zero capital for inventory purposes, you can set up your business and begin trading with customers located just about anywhere around the world.

3. No fulfillment or shipping worries: As an online trader, you would ordinarily be packaging goods and products then shipping these out to your customers. This can be very challenging because shipping is costly and tedious, while the logistics aspect can be overwhelming. Fortunately, under the dropshipping model, this challenge and included cost are eliminated.

4. Test and sell more products with little risk: Unlike numerous other businesses, you are able to update your inventory list without constraints or associated costs. Let us assume that a certain product is doing really well in the market and you wish to benefit from its popularity. It is easy to include such a product into your portfolio of products and make it available to your consumers. Dropshipping allows you this luxury which, in return, earns you more profits in the long run.

Other pros of dropshipping

You do not need to be concerned about space or cost necessary for storing products, which makes it possible to sell as much as you can.

It is possible to operate your business location from practically any location as long as there is an internet connection.

The chances of products getting lost during shipping are cut to almost zero because products are shipped directly from the supplier to your customers.

You do not need to pay allegiance to any inventory items. Any products that are not selling well can be removed and others that are performing better can be added.

There is a lot of time saved since you do not have to process orders and ship out items. You can use this time to scale and improve your website or update your blog and reply to email messages.

The cons of dropshipping

1. Less control over fulfillment: As a trader, you are denied control over lead times and order fulfillment. This means that while you do not shoulder the burden of warehouse stocking, it is going to cost you should a customer be unhappy.

Also, sometimes, the fulfillment partner may mess up orders and this will cost you the trader. Dealing with disappointed customers is never pleasant because for one, you will lose money, and then you will also lose customers. Therefore, always make sure that you partner with reliable and effective dropshipping partners.

2. Shipping Can be Expensive: One of the major challenges of dropshipping is the vague or hidden cost of shipping. You do not stand to benefit from bulk pricing which tends to make shipping much cheaper. As a result, a lot of your earnings are "eaten" or used up in shipping products to customers. To be profitable, you will need to sell a lot more products to make good profits.

3. Reliance on a fulfillment partner: While having a fulfillment partner with their own inventory and warehouse saves you on costs, it can be costly to you in other ways. One reason is that you do not control the inventory, then when stock runs out, you will not be able to accept orders. This can cost you customers and profits. It also leads to much longer lead times, which is not good for your business.

4. Poor customer service: Now, should your fulfillment partners be unreliable, then you are likely to suffer the consequences. For instance, if they send packages late, or deliver wrong items, then the customers will definitely blame you. This is because they do not know about the fulfillment process. All they understand is that they purchased products at your website and items never arrived, were late, or received wrong items.

Also, you will not be able to have that personal touch with your customers mainly because someone else will manage the inventory fulfillment operations for you. Again, the speed at which you will be able to deal with customer challenges is not as fast as it should be.

You can expect to experience some challenges when you act as the person in the middle. This is true, especially if your suppliers or fulfillment partners are too slow. Customers often get annoyed at such antics and will abandon your store for a more reliable one.

These cons can be fixed overtime and it is important to realize that you can learn to either make sure they don't happen or insure they don't happen as regularly! Trial and error is key and getting a mentor to fast track your success will help immensely!

How to Make Dropshipping Easier

While dropshipping has its own share of challenges, Shopify owners have made things a little easier for you. In Shopify, there is a tool designed to make dropshipping work for you.

One of these tools is a cloud-based inventory management program. This software connects you with your suppliers or fulfillment partners so that you are always aware of the availability of inventory items. This way, you will be able to synchronize your marketing campaigns with the stock that is available.

This is just one of the reasons why Shopify is highly recommended.

You should focus on getting an inventory management system that is able to track stock levels in real time. This way, you will minimize and possibly eliminate a lot of the challenges that ordinary dropshippers experience on a regular basis.

Best Dropshipping Niches to Choose from

Choosing a niche should be among your very first steps as you venture into this lucrative online trading mode. It is also among the most crucial steps because it could either make your business or break it. Therefore, approach this process with a lot of due consideration.

There are different approaches that you can use to find the most appropriate niches and brands or products for your online store. One of these is an online service that helps you with market research. What you need to with such software is to enter a product name and the software will then conduct a search and provide you with all the metrics and details pertaining to that particular product. The metrics include average selling price, cost of shipping, and so on.

Another tried and tested approach of product identification is to make use of completed listings at eBay. eBay is one of the most popular and most successful online marketplaces. Therefore, any product that does well on this platform is likely to thrive on other platforms.

There are advanced search tools as well as other features available that you can utilize to conduct a search using your preferred keywords. You will receive a list of both successful and poorly performing products in a given category or niche. A successful product sells 60% or more all the time.

You may already have a following around a certain niche, or know some who does that you can drive that traffic to your product. This is the time where you research deeply and also think widely towards whether you can get free traffic towards your product.

Define Your Products

It is crucial that you accept that no online trader is able to sell everything. Choosing a niche market provides you with one of the best opportunities of setting yourself apart from the competition. It is possible to think that selling a wider variety of products to the general population is a great idea. However, this is not. Online customers have become very specific in what they want and always search for one provider who is knowledgeable about their niche.

Therefore, identify a niche and find suitable products that are in high demand and belong to your chosen niche. It is advisable to only sell a couple of major products than numerous irrelevant ones. This is great for generating quality traffic to your online store. Be specific and be relevant.

Customers are likely to be attracted to your store and accept your brand story if you focus only on a small number of products. Any brand story that you put across is likely not to be believed and will be less convincing if customers get overwhelmed by numerous products available. Your store will become just another online shop and many customers will keep away.

There are certain factors that you should consider when choosing a suitable product. Here is a look at some of these factors:

- Find good quality products that are functional and well designed.
- Identify a product that actually solves a problem that people have.
- Select a product that allows you to add large margins – your aim at this point is to make about 30% gross profit.

Finally, choose a product that will also sell well over the internet. Avoid all unreasonable items such as large, heavy, costly products that require specialized care or unique shipping arrangements.

How to Identify your Niche

Starting your own business is important, but identifying a suitable niche is probably the most crucial decision that you will make. When you start your business and put in the hard work to get it started, you need to make sure that your chosen niche and products have a market and without many competitors. You need to also identify a few niches that you are interested in and then proceed to choose one. You can also expand your thinking level to finding products that are trending. For example when the fidget spinners and hover boards came out, whoever made a dropshipping store while they were still trending killed it!

Dropshipping take a required skill to think outside the box and look from the outside perspective.

Here are some basic steps that you should follow in order to find a Product to Sell:

1. Brainstorm some niche ideas

You should focus on a specific niche, especially one that you are particularly keen on. One of the best decisions you can make is to focus on a smaller subset of the market. For instance, think about selling to vegetarians, yoga lovers, or cross-fit fans. This way, you will easily be able to meet the needs of your customers.

2. Run an Amazon search

One excellent method of finding products that are in great demand is to use Amazon search. The search results will show you, which are the popular niches and the products that do well in these niches. Simply just look at the Amazon.com best sellers and go through the product categories. This is a great way to find what is just popular in general and even what could be trending.

3. Search using Google Keyword Planner

Google Keyword Planner is a powerful tool that will inform you about the number of searches conducted on its search engine regarding a particular niche. This way, it will be possible to discover which among the most lucrative niches are with high demand products.

4. Social Media Research

You should also conduct a niche search across popular social media sites. Examples of these include Instagram, Reddit, YouTube, Twitter, Quora, and Facebook. When you do this, you will find out how other firms are faring, including your potential competitors. You are also likely to come across social influencers or brand influencers with large followers and huge audiences within your chosen niche.

5. Choose your Niche

Now that you have all this information, you are fully equipped and informed to wisely identify a niche. There are a number of excellent niches available, so find one which you can build your business around. The rest of the data that you have should be stored for future reference just in case you may need to switch niches.

The Process of Setting up a Dropshipping Business

1. Identify your Product

Now that you have identified your preferred niche, it is time to set up your dropshipping business. At this stage, you need to search for and identify suitable suppliers who stock the kind of products you wish to deal in. Sometimes, there is a wide variety of suppliers and wholesalers to work with, but in some niches, you may be limited in your choice.

2. Find a supplier

Even at this stage, you will also need to use search engines such as Google to identify wholesalers that deal in products within your niche. You will be searching for suppliers who have a good reputation of being reliable and who price their products in a manner that allows you sufficient margins to be profitable. This step will be examined more closely at a later stage.

3. Establish your brand

Now is the best time to introduce your brand to the world. It is crucial that you establish your brand early enough so that it guides your business and company. There are a couple of things that you can consider. These include a name for your brand. When you have a catchy, memorable, and reasonable brand name, your customers will easily be able to identify it and will always associate your business with the brand.

Now come up with a tagline – a tagline is basically a summary of the unique value proposition of your business. For instance, think of the slogan "Just Do It", by Nike. This slogan is simple yet powerful. It tells you what the company is all about and what it offers. As an athlete, you will be inspired by such a tagline.

Design a logo – A well-designed logo is advisable because it is a visual representation of your brand. There are templates that you can use to make yourself a quality logo for your brand. These can be found at sites such as www.creativemarket.com.

Choose a color pallet – One of the factors that you really need to focus on is to ensure that your website is consistent through and through, especially the color code. It is advisable that you create an atmosphere and rhyme on your website, and colors do this very well. Therefore, choose your colors wisely. For more ideas and advice, check out www.grasshopper.com.

Create an About Us page – You should create a page known as About Us. This is usually the first stop of most visitors, especially when they want to find out more about you. Use this opportunity to tell people your story and your brand. Let them get to know your passion and give them a chance to identify with your business. The story should then extend to your social media sites and onto your advertisements and marketing messages.

The About Us section is where you need to sell yourself. To sell yourself, you must relate to your customer and create likeability. Being detailed with your story and creating likeability with those who read it will keep customers on your site and expand your brand following on social media platforms etc.

The Dropshipping Process

If you have a dropshipping website with a specific brand or a couple of products that you are selling, then customers are likely to visit sooner or later. Therefore, you need to be prepared.

If you choose to sell smartphone accessories, then you can expect plenty of mobile phone users out there to visit your website. A lot of smartphone owners search for e-commerce websites in order to view the different kinds of accessories available.

Sooner or later, a customer known as Mary visits your website and places an order for an accessory. She chooses a charger and pays for it. Once the order is placed, a chain of events takes place. First, an order is completed with all specifications and details sent to the shipping partner.

An email is then sent to Mary confirming her purchase as well as receipt of payment. A payment will also be sent to the dropshipping partner to pay for the cost of the mobile phone charger and the cost of shipping.

Thereafter, the fulfillment company will process the order, acknowledge receipt of payment and ship the product to Mary. You will also receive an email message letting you know that the goods have been dispatched to Mary.

Point to note: It is important to note that as the dropshipper, you do not lift a finger in the processing of the customer's order. All that happens is dispatching of emails and generation of a tracking number which is provided to the customer.

How to Setup your Own Dropshipping Store

Setting up your own brand new store can be both exhilarating and scary. You'd be excited because of the thought of achieving success and becoming profitable. The worry comes from the thought of failing. Even seasoned entrepreneurs often worry about different things such as what could happen if things go wrong.

1. Choosing a brand name

When starting your own online stores, one of the first things you will need to do is to come up with the store's name. This is the name that your customers will become familiar with and share with their friends. It is also the same name that people will enter into search engines.

When creating a brand name, you should come up with a catchy one. This means a name that people will like and will relate with. Also, think about an SEO-optimized name. The name should be aligned with your bigger plan for the brand.

While it can be rather challenging to come up with a reasonable brand name, websites like Oberlo have a business name generator tool that you can use. This tool gives you a wide variety of options to choose from and modify in order to come up with a real business name.

2. Open a Shopify account

If you wish to be a successful dropshipper, then you should open an account with Shopify. It is one of the leading dropshipping platforms and makes it very easy to get started and become successful. The firm has set everything up including plugins, as well as numerous relationships with manufacturers, warehousing partners, and shipping companies.

Some of the numerous benefits of dropshipping with Shopify include selling as many products as you'd like, detecting any fraudulent activity on your account, offer discount codes to your customers, edit images, process customer orders with ease, and a lot more.

3. Set up your own store

You are, at this stage, ready to set up your own dropshipping store. The process is simple and straightforward. First, go to Shopify's sign up page and open an account. You will need to answer a bunch of very easy questions, and once you finish this step, your account should be ready. You will officially become a store owner.

As soon as your store is set up, all you will need to do is complete a couple of steps before you eventually start selling. You will need to choose a theme, install it then work on your Homepage, Layout style, and Product page. Finally, work on your social media pages and advertise on different platforms to let all your friends and everyone else about your brand and store. Finally, come up with a blog and engage your readers and customers on a regular basis. Provide them with information and answer any questions they may have.

Potential Investment

While it is good to spend what is necessary in order to set your business off to a great start, you really do not need to spend that much. What you need to put aside is simply money for your website, for some images, and simple basics like these. At the highest end of the scale, you may spend up to $1000 just to get started, even though numerous entrepreneurs spend much less than that.

Take for instance Shopify, the world's most popular dropshipping website. They will charge you only a small monthly fee. Depending on the package that you choose, you could end up paying as little as $29 per month. If you are great with designs and can follow instructions, then you can design your own store, import images, use add-ons, plug-ins and so on. Someone else may charge you for this, but basically, the entire process is pretty straightforward. According to Oberlo, the average storeowner on Shopify spends about $500 in order to get started.

If you do not have any money then don't just tell yourself you can't start a dropshipping store. This is the time where you reach out and sort out deals. For example you could find someone who would be willing to let you do the work, using their money for the investment. This is where you could both agree to cut the business profits at for example: 60- 40.

5 Mistakes People Make with Dropshipping

While dropshipping does sound like a pretty simple business concept, many people still get some aspects wrong. When you make mistakes, it may cost you a lot. It is absolutely crucial that you consider each step of setting up your business carefully. If you fail to do this, then you might not be profitable and yours will become just another online store.

1. Insufficient brand display

When it comes to dropshipping, maintaining visibility of your brand can be a serious challenge. However, you have to ensure that your customers and general visitors to your online store get to view your brand. Band visibility should be maintained on as numerous places as possible. Find as many things to brand as possible. These include stickers, packing slips and so on. If you appropriately brand yourself, then customers will remember your brand name and any potential customers will search for you by name.

2. Posting overly-optimistic shipping times

Shipping can be a huge challenge for dropshippers because you are not in control of the process. Customers prefer shorter delivery times but are unwilling to pay a premium for this. Shippers, on the other hand, place wide-ranging estimates like 10 to 30 days.

Since customers dislike long waiting times, a business owner may choose to misinform the customer and claim shorter delivery times. Sometimes, these are much shorter than shippers are able to attain. This will cause a problem and customers will think you are unreliable. As the business owner, you should place an order yourself on your own website and see how long the shipping time is.

3. Unrealistic expectations

It is a fact that dropshipping is a potentially lucrative business. There are hundreds of traders across the world earning large profits from this business model. However, it does not mean that you will start earning a five-figure amount within the first one or even three months.

When you start off with such high expectations, you may end up disappointed. Dropshipping is a venture that requires time and effort, as well as plenty of learning before serious profits start coming your way. You need to learn how to set realistic expectations. Expect modest earnings at first or even zero earnings for a month or two. Things should then pick up slowly and within a short time, you should be doing great.

4. Offering a variety of shipping fees

Sometimes a dropshipper may offer a variety of shipping fees as offered by different shipping companies. However, this has the possibility of complicating your website with numerous options. Your customers may also get confused because what they really want is the cheapest and fastest shipping option available.

A good solution to this problem is to charge no shipping fees. Opt for a free shipping model which is way more attractive with reduced logistics. Alternatively, you can offer a flat shipping fee if you need to offer a faster shipping time. This way, your customers will have a choice between free shipping that takes longer or a shipping fee which means faster shipping times.

5. Competing on price

It may seem lucrative to lower your prices and beat the competition. While this may sound like a nice business move, it really isn't. Having a competitive price is not sustainable in the long term. The profit margins in dropshipping are pretty low and any price cut will eat into your profits.

Scaling Up Your Dropshipping Business

When you have an online business that is operating successfully, one of your major goals will be to scale it up. You will be seeking to scale your business even as revenues rise. However, you may encounter some challenges. For instance, you may experience a large influx of orders and fulfillment requirements. It is crucial to establish that you have the resources, financial, time, and so on, to handle the expected growth.

It is easier to scale up as a dropshipper compared to an ordinary online trader. The latter will have to hire additional help which can be costly compared to the rate of return. However, as a dropshipper, you will only have to ensure that your dropshipping partner is handling the orders on time. If they become overwhelmed, then you may need an additional supplier.

Product testing: Another way of scaling up your store is to introduce more products. However, there is always a challenge when it comes to new products. You may not be sure where to begin and a possible solution is products testing. Entrepreneurs often add products to their shelves which do not sell very well.

Entrepreneurs often have to keep trying and testing different products until they find the ones that work. Therefore, find products that sell well and make the part of your portfolio.

Long-tail products: You can choose to sell some long-tail products on your website as well. These are products that sell in low volumes, but the profit margins are pretty good. Also, think about selling seasonal products like Halloween and Christmas products. These can include costumes, cards, and decorations and so on.

Adding such products will not just provide your regular customers with products and services, but will also attract new customers. This way, you will always be earning a little extra and will enjoy returns throughout the year. There are various ways of scaling up your business, so keep trying different methods and see which methods work the best for you.

Chapter 3: Amazon FBA

Amazon, one of the world's largest e-commerce companies, has come up with an advanced and useful fulfillment service that allows businesses to grow, thrive, and gain their customer's trust. This arrangement allows sellers to store their products at Amazon fulfillment centers.

Basically, under the Amazon Fulfillment program, you will be required to identify stores where you want your products stored. Once orders are placed by customers on Amazon's website, Amazon fulfillment services will pick up the product, pack it and ship it to the customer.

Amazon also provides customer services for all its FBA clients and delivers an excellent customer experience. As a trader, you need to make use of this service to increase your customer numbers, reach a wider population, and increase your profitability.

Pros and Cons of Amazon FBA

Advantages

One of the major advantages of using Amazon FBA is that it saves you time. Whenever an order comes in, you do not have to process it as all processing and fulfillment is performed by Amazon. This way, you are left with a lot of free time which you can then spend doing other important things.

All products on Amazon FBA are eligible for Amazon's prime shipping. This means that your products are eligible for Amazon's two-day and even one-day shipping. Amazon Prime members who buy your products will enjoy this service anytime they buy your products.

Another advantage of using Amazon FBA is that Amazon fulfillment will process orders originating not just from their website but from other channels as well, such as your business website. Your customers can place orders on other platforms as well as Amazon will fulfill these orders.

Customers are happy with Amazon's professional service. Amazing has been in the e-commerce place for numerous years and has become a leading provider of professional fulfillment services.

Also, the entire process is easy and economical. You only pay when you use the service. You also get to pay storage charges for goods in Amazon's stores and the cost of shipping. However, there are no additional charges and all charges are known upfront.

You can also sell your products on other platforms such as eBay without any hustle. Simply join the Amazon FBA program and they will enable the multi-channel selling so that you have access to customers across multiple platforms.

Therefore, you get a chance to sell in large volumes while Amazon takes charge of all returns. You get to bundle and multi-pack your items in order to fetch even better deals. And since shipping can be costly and sometimes complicated, it is advisable to use Amazon and let the firm use its experience with shipping and customs.

Disadvantages

There are certain disadvantages or cons of using Amazon FBA. The main challenge of using this service is the cost involved. The costs can significantly eat into your profits.

Another disadvantage has to do with the mingling of products. Your inventory items will be sorted with other similar products which means its possible that a customer may receive an item that you did not send to Amazon.

Sometimes it can be tricky to determine exact volume quantities that you need to store at Amazon outlets. This is true, especially during holiday seasons. You may overstock and pay for unnecessary storage or under-stock and miss out on sales.

You need patience because it might take a while before your products start selling. During this time, you will be incurring costs because your products will be in stores but with no customers yet.

Also, Amazon FBA is a great idea if you are a full-time trader. You can make sufficient profits if it is your fulltime occupation. However, if you only sell part-time, then you are unlikely to succeed using this model because your costs will be high will income remains low.

Getting Started with Amazon FBA

If you wish to build a successful online business that is profitable and generates a good income, then consider signing up for Amazon FBA. There are a couple of steps that you need to make if you are to be successful. The first step is to identify a suitable niche.

1. Find a profitable niche

One of the first steps you need to take is to identify a profitable product or niche on Amazon. You really need to identify a profitable niche if you are to become profitable. An option that you really should consider as a beginner is what is known as private labeling. Under this approach, you take a successful product that is doing well and change its label. You need to add your own label to the successful product and then make it available at Amazon.

As an entrepreneur, you do not really need to invent a new product. There are thousands of manufacturers and suppliers out there who have products that are already thriving. They will be happy to partner with you so that you sell even more of their products. This approach is the easiest one for most beginners.

One of the best ways of finding products that sell best on Amazon is to visit its best-seller list at www.amazon.gp.bestseller. Check this website out and you will see all the different products and niches that sold really well in the past year.

2. Find a manufacturer or supplier to private label your chosen items

As soon as you determine the products that you will sell on Amazon FBA, the next step is to identify a manufacturer or a supplier who will private label products for you. There are to basic ways of identifying potential suppliers. The first is to use Google's search engine to identify US-based manufacturers. The next is to use Alibaba at www.alibaba.com. It is crucial that you identify as many suppliers and manufacturers as possible for your products.

You need to find out as much as possible about your potential suppliers including details about who is behind the firm, the manufacturer, where they are located and so on. You also need to ask for sample products before placing an order with your chosen one. If the product samples are good enough for Amazon, then go ahead and identify the most suitable supplier.

3. Create your own packaging, product label, and graphics

Now that you have identified the ideal product that you wish to sell, the next step is to create your own brand. What you need to do is come up with your own product graphics, packaging, and product labeling. You only do this once you have identified a suitable partner to work with.

As you do this, think about coming up with your own brand name and a logo. These will go a long way in establishing your product as a known and trusted brand. There are certain places that you can go to get your brand designed. These include www.Fiverr.com, Upwork, and 99Designs. When you come up with your own brand, you will be able to sell multiple products to a wide customer base and establish yourself as a reliable and trustworthy brand.

4. Send your products to Amazon and start selling

Once your logo, packaging, and brand are ready, you should send complete products to Amazon. Send the products to the stores that you want or believe will serve you the best. Remember that the US is Amazon's largest market so think about selling here first and take advantage of millions of these customers. Also, ensure that you set up an Amazon Seller account. Choose the professional account and start selling. At the same time, you will want to come up with an Amazon product listing.

5. Begin the marketing process

At this point, all that you need to do is begin marketing your products and brand on various platforms. You should market and promote your brand an enable it to rank in Amazon and other search engines so that you start getting sales.

Finding Amazon FBA Niches on Alibaba

There are over 1,000 low competition niche products that you can sell on Amazon FBA. A niche is basically a closely defined market sector with some traits that are very similar. Traits could be demographics, location, common interest, and problem and so on.

The best approach to finding a profitable niche is actually identifying a niche with sufficient demand but limited competition. If you can identify such a niche, then you will be on the pathway to success. To achieve this, you need to focus on the following points;

- *Sufficient demand:* This is determined by the number of customers that are searching for a particular product. A good product is one that sells roughly 5 – 10 products

- *Not very competitive:* You will be searching to find a product that is obscure enough to not attract too much competition

One of the first places to head to if you are searching for online communities and forums is Reddit. Reddit is the front-page of the internet. If anything new or popular is discovered, then Reddit will be the place that it is mentioned, analyzed, discussed, and dissected. This platform is a fun and exciting place where participants form "subreddits" or niches. Getting into a "subreddit" is a great way of identifying an exciting and financially lucrative niche.

Alibaba: Alibaba can become a crucial partner and source of quality but cheap products. Search for suppliers of the product or niche that you are in. when you search on Alibaba, keep a close eye on product volumes and price.

Customers will choose your product over others most probably because of a lower price. However, never opt to simply lower your prices because others will do the same and you will all eventually lose out.

If you wish to seriously sell profitably at Amazon, then you need to ensure that you actually stand out from the competition. If you sell the same product as everyone else, you may enjoy only short-lived gains. These, however, won't last. For purposes of successful selling on Amazon FBA, you need to improve on already successful items.

Characteristics of an ideal Amazon FBA product:

- The product should be small in size and light in weight
- It can sell over 500 units per month

- The niche is not dominated by a major brand
- Product is not fragile
- Product is not seasonal
- It is simple and non-electronic
- It is non-patented and has no trademarks
- Item is priced between $12 and $55

While there are numerous tools out there that can be used for product research, the ideal approach would be to search through Amazon's catalog in order to identify the unique and stand out products that have a lower number of reviews.

In brief, when you identify an excellent niche, ensure that it is one with high sales volumes but low levels of competition. Find a product or products in this niche that sell well. Look at the negative reviews and then identify a product on Alibaba that solves the problems raised by users. This "reverse engineering" approach of improving an otherwise successful product will lead you to great success especially if you can find a great supplier.

The following is a list of top five niches that have seen huge success in 2018.

1. Books – hardcopies. A lot of people were of the impression that books had gone never to reappear. However, it is interesting to note that not only are books still around but are actually selling very well.

2. Baby products: There is still a huge demand for children's products even though this demand has been there for decades. For as long as human beings continue to procreate, then the demand for baby products such as toys will continue to grow.

3. Jewelry: Items that glitter such as gold, jewelry, gems, and other precious metals still actually sell on Amazon. They appear to be constantly in demand and the profits can be pretty attractive. However, you have to be a super diligent seller to sell jewelry successfully for the long term.

4. Workout clothing and accessories: A lot of people apparently enjoy working out and keeping fit. And these people purchase plenty of workout wear. It is among the top sellers at Amazon and there is room for additional sellers to join the fray. And the best part is that most buyers usually buy new and never second-hand workout clothing.

5. Electronic items and accessories: People love tech gadgets and they spend billions of dollars on these gadgets each year. Think about electronics that people buy often and then identify products within the niche that fit this profile.

How to Setup an Amazon FBA Business

Amazon is the largest online retailer in the US, UK, and Europe. It is also one of the largest online retailers in the world. The term FBA stands for fulfillment by Amazon. This means that businesses that sign up for Amazon FBA will have their products stored at Amazon's warehouses with all orders processed and shipped by the retailer.

Amazon FBA does not handle the storage and fulfillment aspects but also the customer service. This frees you up to do other things that you like. Also, when you do not have to worry about warehousing and storage, you will be able to focus more on building your brand and business. Amazon FBA allows your small business to act as a large corporation by leveraging on Amazon's huge customer base and wide reach.

First step: Create your own Amazon seller account

The first step that you should take is to create an Amazon seller account. Opening an account is definitely the first step if you want to sell on Amazon. There are two basic types of sellers on Amazon. These are amateurs and professionals. Amateurs pay no monthly fees but professionals are charged a fee of about $39.99 per month exclusive of selling fees.

Identify a product and establish your private label

One of the best approaches of selling on Amazon's FBA platform is through private labeling. The idea behind it is to give you a chance to build your own brand. Basically, you will establish your own label or brand and then sell branded products on Amazon.

There is a whole process of searching for products to sell on Amazon. Make sure that you carefully consider the products that you will sell so they are popular and sell in large volumes.

Source products

You will need to source your products from somewhere. A lot of people are sourcing products from Alibaba. It has become a super simple process. Sellers are buying unbranded products on Alibaba, labeling them, and then marking up the price. You should learn how to perform appropriate research. Do your research on both Amazon and Alibaba marketplaces. Amazon results will teach you about the best selling products and top niches while Alibaba will show you the products that you need to buy and brand.

Get your products to Amazon from Alibaba

Once you find the products that you wish to sell, you will need to acquire them from Alibaba and transfer them to Amazon stores. There are plenty of firms in the logistics arena that will be happy to partner with you and ship your goods at an affordable rate. Freight forwarders such as Flex Port can provide you with shipping services.

Pricing and marketing

You will be surprised at how cheap products actually are on Alibaba. This might present you with a challenge of appropriate pricing. It is not as simple as just adding a markup because there are plenty of costs involved. You should work out the price professionally and the best approach would be to use professional calculators such as the one offered by Amazon. Using this calculator known as the profitability calculator from Amazon, you will easily come up with the appropriate price as recommended by Amazon.

The final stage is marketing. You need to get out there and start marketing and advertising your products and brand. Since you will have a lot of time on your hands, you should focus this time on your marketing efforts. Start by optimizing your products so they rank well on search engines. You should then proceed to market on different platforms including popular social media as well as a personal blog. These are proven ways that have worked in the past and continue to be effective.

How to Product-Launch on Amazon FBA

Amazon loves it when a seller brings in traffic from outside. In fact, Amazon rewards sellers who attract sales and traffic by strategically listing them on predominant searches.

A product launch is a process that is designed to help your product launch on the first page of search results for major keyword phrases and keywords relating to your product. The launch consists of promotional giveaways for purposes of increasing sales volumes and improving keyword ranking on Amazon. When your keywords rank higher, you are able to attract more clicks, impressions, and sales. The goal of the process is to ensure that your listings also appear in organic search results in order to increase organic sales.

Steps of launching your products on Amazon FBA

- Create a landing page away from Amazon. The page should include your offer and listing. This is faster and cheaper compared to other platforms.

- Reserve an inventory for your FBA
- Come up with a promotion campaign
- Create social media campaigns for Facebook and others
- Make sure that you have a follow-up plan

1. Create your own landing page

Take your leading product or brand and then create a suitable landing page on a platform of choice. You can consider a platform such as www.mysellerpal.com or any other. Make sure that the page contains suitable content including the name of the item, images of the product, current price and other useful information. There is often a promo code or some other form of discount because of the launch. Include this on your landing page to entice members to buy from you.

2. Use an FBA multi-channel to reserve your FBA inventory

Make sure that you reserve your inventory not just for Amazon but also for other outlets. Fortunately, it is possible to sell across different platforms including eBay and your own website. At a later date, you could free up your multichannel fulfillment order from Amazon in order to free up your inventory.

3. Come up with a promo code for Amazon users

It is easy to create a promo code for Amazon users. When you do this, ensure that its single-use code one per customer. The aim is to provide your first customers with a discount when they buy your product. When they buy, they will likely to share their positive experiences with others who will then be inspired to become customers of your products.

4. Advertise on social media

You really need to extend your marketing campaigns to social media. You need to identify your target market and let them know about the product, the launch date, promo codes, and all other benefits. Popular social media include YouTube, Facebook, and Instagram.

As a seller, you will benefit from the launch in the following ways;

- The launch will increase your sales volumes and velocity
- It will boost your keyword ranking
- Your product will get more authority on Amazon
- Improves organic traffic for a better conversion rate

Financing necessary to get you started

So how much money do you need in order to get established on Amazon FBA? The full amount will depend on exactly what you want and how you choose to implement your product.

Product costs

There are other costs that you may want to get out of the way first. One of these is the product cost. This will probably be the biggest cost that you will incur. There are plenty of products available so your costs here will depend on your choice of product.

Experts recommend acquiring between 400 to 500 units just to get started. If each product costs between $2 and $5 then your total product cost will be between $800 and $2,500.

Shipment costs

Shipment costs will also vary. The variation will depend on factors such as weight, volume, and distance. When it comes to Amazon, the costs will also depend on whether you are sourcing products from the US or from Alibaba. You can expect to pay an average of 30 – 50% of your product costs in shipping and handling charges. If we paid $2,100 for our product and fees cost 30% of the total, then you will have to pay 30% * 2100 = $630.

Research tools

You will have to use some tools to do your product research. Most of these tools are free but some are quite costly. If you use some of the best tools in the market, then you can expect to pay about $30.

Other costs

You can expect to pay a few other expenses. These include $39.99 for an Amazon professional account, logo and branding at about $40, and $100 for UPC barcode. You could have a few additional costs such as photography $100 and another $100 for inspections. Your total initial bill will then come to;

Total amount = $2,000+$630+$30+$39.99+$40+$100+$100 = **$2,940**

8 Mistakes People Make with Amazon FBA

1. Disregarding the guidelines

Selling on Amazon is a very simple process. This is, in fact, what attracts lots of new sellers onto this platform. However, a lot of these new sellers do not pay head to Amazon's policies. A lot of sellers wake up only to find their accounts suspended or even banned. The reason this happens is that sellers disregard basic rules. You need to read Amazon's policies, follow the rules, and abide by their instructions and guidelines.

2. Insufficient funds to maintain an account

There are plenty of sellers who open Amazon FBA accounts but without a long-term plan. Many run into trouble when they can no longer afford to pay operating fees for their accounts. Others encounter financial challenges and are unable to meet their financial obligations.

Remember that having sufficient funds to buy stock and get it to storage is not enough. You still need to buy new stock once the old one is almost depleted. You also need to take action almost immediately. Therefore, ensure that there is some money set aside just in case you need additional stock especially because sometimes it takes Amazon a couple of weeks to transfer your money into your account.

3. Not doing sufficient product research

It is possible when you first start selling on Amazon that your initial products will not do that well. The main cause of this is usually insufficient research. You need to do sufficient research if you are to successfully sell on Amazon.

4. Not learning about restrictions and barriers within your niche market

There are certain products and niches that require approvals before selling. When it comes to such products, you will have to submit proper documentation including invoices before selling. Sometimes you may have to pay some upfront fees to get approved. This can be disastrous should it happen to you. Therefore, always find out as much information about your product and niche before signing up.

5. Getting low-quality products

If you want to sell products under a private label on Amazon, you must make sure that these are of the best quality. You simply cannot afford to sell low or poor quality products because your customers will not come back. All it takes to kill your business are a couple of negative reviews from disgruntled customers. Therefore, take the time to find good quality products and pay a little extra if you have to.

6. Acquiring costly products for your niche

Be very careful when it comes to pricing. There are plenty of hidden costs and charges when it comes to private labels. There are sourcing costs, shipping, promotions, advertising, shipping, and numerous others. Fortunately, there are tools available that can help you come up with the ideal price for your products. The Amazon FBA Calculator is one such tool that you can effectively use to arrive at the best price for your brand.

7. Sourcing a patented product

When searching for private label products, one of the things that you need to keep an eye out for is patents. Are the products you want to sell patented? It happens sometimes that sellers will actually have patented products manufactured and sold on Amazon. This can cause serious challenges in the future and a lawsuit or claims may be filed against you.

8. Violating terms of service

Unfortunately, a lot of companies and individuals play dirty when it comes to reviews. They tend to adopt black hat tactics that are against the terms of service of Amazon. Most of this activity involves generating false negative reviews. This is strictly against Amazon's policies and they do monitor comments diligently. If you engage in comment manipulation, then Amazon will soon catch up with you and you will probably be heavily penalized.

How to Scale up your Amazon FBA Business

If you want to scale up your Amazon FBA business, then there are a couple of factors that you need to watch out for. Like many others, you probably want to grow a sustainable business that will reward you financially for many years to come. However, if you want to beat the competition and stay at the top, then you need to do the following;

- *Stay on top of the numbers*

To be a successful trader, you need to sell products in large volumes and make a decent profit out of it. You really need to be on top of your numbers especially the vital ones. Avoid the non-vital ones such as gross sales as these may mislead you. Focus more on volume, profit margins, and net profit.

- *Construct a website*

A website is a crucial platform for your brand. While you do not need a website to begin selling on Amazon, having one is definitely beneficial to your business. It enables you to boost your online presence and also gives you an opportunity to scale up your brand and business.

Also, building a website allows you space to expand your online presence on a website that belongs to you. A website gives you the kind of flexibility that you do not have on Amazon. You can sell products from your website and have Amazon FBA fulfill orders from your site.

- *Improve your best seller ranking*

One of the best ways of improving your ranking on the best seller list is simply to outsell your competitors. Even then, this is easier said than done. There are certain factors that determine your ranking on the bestseller list. These include boosting your hourly sales, making use of the correct keywords, request more reviews of your Amazon page and also make use of enticing photos and better product descriptions.

- *Find a competitive advantage over others*

If you want to grow and scale up, then you should find a competitive advantage over other sellers. This is usually something that you are able to do that others cannot. For instance, some of the more successful sellers on Amazon usually have better marketing plans while others work hard on building relationships. For instance, if you are selling kitchenware then it makes sense to befriend a celebrated chef or a trusted food blogger.

- *Have a good system in place*

If you want to scale up your business, you need to have an excellent system in place. It is the systems and processes that you adopt that will enable you to scale up and grow. It is understandable that you will not want to employ workers to perform some of the services for you. However, having a scalable system is advisable. This includes making use of the correct tools necessary to automate most of the processes.

Some of the processes that you can automate include keyword and rank tracking, product re-pricing, accounting, and marketing.

Chapter 4: Affiliate Marketing

An Introduction To Affiliate Marketing

We can define affiliate marketing as the process of promoting other businesses products or services and earning a percentage of any resulting sales. This approach of earning a passive income is pretty popular as over 81% of major brands surveyed in a study claimed to be using it.

The income derived from affiliate marketing is considered as passive income because you make the money without actively participating in customer service, promotion platform, delivery and everything else that goes with providing a service or product. Instead, all you have to do is get people to buy through your affiliate link. essentially driving traffic to that link is all you need to do. You live your life, go about your business and only put in a little bit of work regularly and earn a passive income.

Affiliate marketing is hugely beneficial. This is the reason why a huge majority of people seeking a passive income always choose this path. There are little entry barriers and takes generally little work before the money starts rolling in. there are certain benefits of this kind of revenue source.

Affiliate marketing over the years

Affiliate marketing was almost everyone's number one destination source for a passive income. It is an approach that works and has delivered for many people. However, over the years, the marketing approach acquired a bad name owing to unscrupulous and dishonest affiliates. Fortunately, a lot of this kind of behavior has been curbed and affiliate marketing is back to being a respected means of earning a living.

A survey of top brands reveals that over 81% of all major brands offer affiliate marketing opportunities. Affiliate marketing is therefore considered a crucial part of the overall marketing strategy of major brands. There are numerous benefits of tapping into this market as the entry barrier is pretty low yet it provides a reliable passive source of income.

Pros and Cons

Why choose affiliate marketing?

There are a couple of reasons why anyone would opt for affiliate marketing. Here is a look at some of the numerous reasons why people opt for this approach and why it is so successful.

- You do not have to create new products or even come up with new content. All you might need to do is to include some affiliate recommendations on content that you already have
- You are free to sign up for as many affiliate programs as possible. You should not be limited to just one or two programs. While this is a great way of promoting products, it also an effective brand exposure method
- Joining is easy with little or no barriers. Anyone seeking to join an affiliate program can easily manage to do so. Leaving such a program is just as easy
- You get to earn a passive income which can greatly boost your income for many years to come

Downsides of affiliate marketing

While there are many great benefits of affiliate marketing, there are a couple of cons. Here is a look at some of the downsides of affiliate marketing.

- The returns are usually pretty small such that you have to have plenty of affiliates offering a decent return.

- You have to be on the lookout for low-quality products as these can harm your online reputation. You should only promote good quality products
- Another problem is spamming when you add too many promotions to your website. This makes it too spammy for your visitors who may not necessarily wish to be bombarded by too many marketing messages
- If you add too many affiliate links to your website, you may harm your SEO rankings and this will definitely hurt your marketing endeavors

Bonus: Selling courses are Key when it comes to Affiliate Marketing. Course Usually give you an affiliate commission on 50%. ALL profit!

Getting Started with Affiliate Marketing

For the most part, affiliate marketing benefits easily outweigh the disadvantages. Affiliate marketing is well suited for blogs and websites that publish content on a regular basis. Internet users are regularly searching for content in the form of information, videos and soon. A blog or website that provides the kind of information these users need constitutes a perfect affiliate marketing partner. The following steps will guide you on how to get started.

1. Think about your website's focus

Affiliate marketing works best when your website focuses or shares' interest with products that are being promoted. This means that your website should be promoting products or services that your readers are interested in. Therefore, you need to be very clear about your chosen niche and the kind of topics and subjects that you cover.

Your website already has a target audience based on the kind of niche you are in. Make sure that you first establish yourself as a guru in your chosen niche so that readers get to trust you. If they believe that you are a subject matter expert, then you will be the one they come to for information and advice. It is then that you can decide to introduce some of the affiliate links that you have signed up to.

As a website owner, think about the kinds of problems your audience has and what kind of solutions your website can provide. Then think about the products or services that can help solve these problems. Also, engage your readers and let them express their thoughts about the problems and challenges they are experiencing. Communicating with readers directly is important as it shows that you care about your readers.

2. Choose your affiliate partners carefully

Basically, once you make a determination regarding your preferred partner, you still need to identify the correct products to promote. You need to be careful when it comes to product selection. If you select a poor quality product then you can expect to make little profit and your customers will probably run away from you.

First, start by only promoting products that you know and have personally used. This way, you will know exactly what you are offering your customers and can vouch for the products.

Next, you will review the terms of the affiliate programs that you sign up to. Some have certain requirements that you may not be in agreement with. Others may provide an easy entry pathway while others may limit your association. Reviewing terms before signing is something you really should not neglect doing.

You should also search for reviews from others using affiliate programs. Find out what the terms were, what the experience was like, and the kind of profits they were making. This way, you will be more informed about what to expect.

If you wish to find ideas about the affiliate programs that you can join, think about the products and services that you use on a regular basis. If you have invaluable experience about some of these products, then consider signing up on any affiliate programs that deal in these products.

3. Design your Website

You can do your affiliate marketing on any website. However, the free platform WordPress offers affiliate marketers a lot more advantages compared to ordinary websites. For instance, you get access to numerous free tools that you can use to help you make the best use of affiliate links. Most of these tools come in the form of plugins which you can use on your WordPress website. A good example of a plugin is Thirsty Affiliates. This is a plugin from WordPress that allows you to add links from your affiliate partners to your website. It also helps you to manage and organize them.

The plugin from WordPress also allows you to track your statistics and add corresponding images. Another plugin is known as Pretty Links. This offers features almost similar to Thirsty Affiliates. However, it focuses more on optimizing your affiliate links. While these are free plugins, they have premium versions with even more features. You also get plenty of alternative options to choose from. Therefore, if you do not have your own website but wish to perform affiliate marketing, then you will be right by choosing WordPress for your affiliate marketing purposes.

4. Come up with high-quality content

Make sure that you create good quality content that is useful and adds value to your reader's lives. Good content needs to be properly researched and well written. If you can, provide different media such as videos and images.

Remember that your readers will not necessarily click on the affiliate links that you provide unless you urge them to. Encourage them to purchase the products and vouch for them based on your knowledge or experience. You can do this successfully if you have high-quality content that helps you to convert readers into customers.

First, you need to demonstrate to your readers how the affiliate product on your website will benefit them or improve their lives. You should then include a call to action that urges them to click on the link and then, where possible, try and provide a complete review of the products you intend to promote.

Finally, take a look at some examples of existing affiliate content. There are some pretty good examples available. Use these examples to inspire you and possibly guide you on how to come up with your own campaign. Affiliate marketing may sound a little challenging but with time it should work out for you. All you need to do is remember are the following steps:

    1. Think about your website's niche and focus
    2. Carefully select your affiliate programs and partners
    3. Identify the tools you need and install them on your website
    4. Now focus on creating quality content and include a variety of media
    5. Market your website, review products that you are promoting and invite your readers to try some of them out

Passive Nature of Affiliate Marketing

Affiliate marketing is passive in nature. The reason is that you do little to no work occasionally. At first, you will have some work to do. For instance, you will need to produce high-quality content which takes a lot of hard work including relevant research.

You will also need to create your own website and probably review some of the products that you will be promoting. Fortunately for most people promoting products and services that you have a passion for seems more like fun than work. Also, when you write about topics that you are passionate about, it feels more like a relaxing task rather than work.

After you get established, you will only do very little work towards marketing and working directly to market the affiliate. Most people spend four hours or less each day working on their affiliate marketing projects. Many others work only a few days each week.

When you put in very little work towards a project that earns you an income, then it becomes a passive source of income. When you work longer than 4 hours, then it ceases to be passive and becomes active.

Best Niches for Affiliate Marketing

Health, wealth, and romance

There are some niches that are always big and always profitable. They include niches such as wealth, health, and romance. Choosing any one of these will provide you with lots of options to blog, write, and promote affiliate products. However, some of these niches have sub-niches.

Take the health sector for instance. We have sub-niches such as quit smoking, weight loss and diet, and embarrassing problems, and so on. It is said that the health and wellness industry is worth over $1 trillion as of 2017. And the smart drug for the brain industry is worth just as much.

Also important to note is that that the diabetes industry in America sees over $322 billion spent each year. This shows that there is a lot of money out there and you can direct some of it to your way through affiliate marketing. Think about other health niches such as the numerous diets out there and so on. there are generally over 50 niches just in the health sector alone.

Other examples in the health sector:

Nootropics
Diabetes recipes
Increasing testosterone
Hair loss
Child obesity
Mole removal
Healthy gut
Insomnia
Weight loss for women
Quit smoking
Stress management
Addictions

Here is where you can do affiliate marketing in the health and wellness sector:

1. Bodybuilding.com – bodybuilding supplements: 15% commission
2. Silver Blade Brands – for males: 40% commissions
3. Kala Health – dietary supplements: 20% commission per sale
4. 88 Herbs – herbal supplements: 18% commission per sale

Niches in the wealth sector

The wealth niche is pretty diverse too. It includes sub-niches such as MLM or multi-level marketing, affiliate marketing, gambling, Forex, internet marketing, and investment opportunities, and so on.

In the UK alone, online business is worth a whopping 100 billion GBP. This amount is double that of the restaurant and hotel industries combined. On the other hand, in the United States, the gambling industry is worth close to $36 billion while the Forex markets have a daily turnover of approximately $5 trillion. All these niches are extremely lucrative.

Additional niche ideas

Online jobs
Amazon FBA
App development
Solar power
Senior living
3D printing

Wealth affiliate websites

Wealthtraders.com/affiliate-program: 40% commission
Bitbond.com/affiliate: 50% commission
Excellerate Associates – 20% commission
Wealth creators club – 45% commission
Trader FX – 20% commission
Surefire Trading – 50% commission
Why you should choose wealth niches

Most wealth niches need subscribers to spend money on services and products. These products range in cost from a few hundreds to thousands of dollars. Also, people are always seeking ways of getting wealthy so they will always keep searching for opportunities. This means more success for you are a marketer. Most of the wealth niches are costly and investors will keep on buying into them hoping for better returns and up-to-date information.

Romance and dating niches

Yet another niche that should interest your because of its evergreen nature is romance and dating. Romance and dating refer to romantic books, online dating, finding a spouse and so much more.

Statistics indicate that more than 49 million Americans have at least once in their lifetime joined a dating website. There are other sub-niches involved such as marriage counseling and so on. There are also books on enhancing marriages and so much more. Some of the more popular niches include:

Seniors dating
Christian dating
Pre-marital counseling

Here are some common affiliate programs

Cupid: you make $135 when an order is placed
Love City: 50% commission
Sexy Confidence: A payout of $99 per sale
E-harmony: Earn $188 each time someone signs up
Commitment connection: You earn 70% commission

Other popular niches for affiliate marketing:

1. High paying affiliate programs such as private jet charters and yacht rentals
2. Hobbies people spend money on such as sports, travel, sailing, golf, cruises

You are likely to be very successful in the niche that you choose. This is because people are pretty desperate for solutions to their problems. Consumers are searching for a magic bullet that will ease their pain and suffering.

Remember that you do not necessarily have to settle down in one affiliate program. You can try and join as many programs as you can to boost your profits. There are numerous affiliate products that you can promote both physical and digital in most of these niches.

There are always new gadgets and equipment that make people happy so activities and hobbies are going to be around for a long time to come. Your strategy could include the creation of an affiliate website, starting a blog, compiling an email list, or any other business model that you find suitable. Also, rich people will always spend their money hoping to create or generate more wealth.

Basically, there is no one single affiliate marketing niche that can be said to be the most profitable. However, if you want to earn some serious profits, then choose one of these three evergreen niches.

Build a Brand for Extra Reach

Branding is a crucial aspect of any business that seeks success. However, this word gets tossed around so much that its meaning gets lost. Basically, at the very basic level, your brand is what your consumers actually know about you. Therefore, your brand refers to your products, image, and reputation.

Therefore, when building your brand, think about your products and the problem that they solve and how they make people feel. As you create your brand, keep in mind that a good brand tells customers what to expect and helps them make major business decisions. A good brand should make customers feel safe and will thereby build trust and confidence in the brand, your company, and in you.

Things to consider when building your brand

1. Culture: Culture refers to an aggregation of beliefs, values, images, ideas, and history. Ideally, all brands fit within a culture and the top brands define a certain aspect of the culture where they exist.

2. Aesthetics: This is when we design a brand such that it is pleasant to look at, feels nice and is attractive to customers. When designing your brand, always think about aesthetics.

3. Position: Brand positioning includes making decisions about your specific customer base, your brand's association with the customers and the kind of marketing awareness you wish to create.

Other attributes that you should also consider include identity, customers, and personality. Once you have your brand properly defined, you can then proceed to market it on different platforms but especially on social media.

Marketing on social media is effective, relatively affordable, and easy to get started. However, if you have no clue about how to go about it, then you had better learn how to. Popular social media such as Facebook, YouTube, and Instagram are very popular and have a wide reach.

Open pages on different platforms, especially the ones mentioned above, then start inviting your friends to like, follow, endorse, and invite others to your page. Add content, including videos, photos, and informative articles about your products and brand. Within no time, you will begin growing your numbers and selling your products.

Potential Investment

It is possible to begin an affiliate marketing career with no money at all. You can start your campaigns with virtually no money and still become successful. However, if you wish to be successful almost from the start, then you may need to invest a small amount of money upfront. Here is a breakdown of the expected costs.

Get a domain name: This will cost you perhaps about $5 only. This amount could be even less on some sites. Your website will need a domain name so getting one is essential.

Hosting services: Your website will need to be hosted somewhere. Hosting charges vary but you can expect to pay about $6 to $10 per month.

Additional costs: You should also spend a little more money to campaign and market your website and products. Think about PPC campaigns, SEO and keyword tools, email marketing, images, and some outsourcing. All these will cost you a lot less than $500.

However, once your website is up and running, most of these costs will not be necessary as many are one-time expenses. You can expect to pay about $120 monthly to maintain your affiliate marketing business. These are costs associated with hosting, maintenance, outsourcing and so on. Once you become profitable, then these costs will be taken care of.

Crucial Mistakes to Avoid

1. Hoping to make money right away

It is near impossible to be profitable at the onset. This is because you are unknown and there is still a lot of marketing and outreach work to do. While it is possible to make some money even at the start, you will hardly be profitable within the first few months.

2. Not collecting emails

One of the most crucial things you need to do from the onset is to start collecting emails. Building an email list is crucial for your marketing campaigns. The reason you need to collect email is that emails bring you the most traffic, more traffic means more sales, and you can keep the list should anything happen to your websites.

3. Choosing a niche with little public interest

One of the biggest mistakes that you could ever make with affiliate marketing is choosing a niche that most people have no interest in. Instead, find a niche that you have an interest in and are passionate about.

4. Producing low-quality content

This is yet another mistake that you should never make. Remember that your customers and readers look up to you as a leader in your chosen field. Ensure that you always produce high-quality content that is informative and easy to understand.

5. Relying largely on Google traffic

Getting traffic from Google to your website is great. However, you should not rely on this source only. Even as you optimize your website, you should source traffic from other sites like your blog and social media.

Remember that Affiliate Marketing is all about driving traffic to your product. So link social media platforms, Google Ads, Word of Mouth. Everything you can. And this will fast track more sales and therefore more returns in your pocket.

Chapter 5: eBay Selling

What is eBay selling?

eBay is a very popular online marketplace where sellers and buyers get together to sell or buy just about anything. If you wish to sell any item, all you need to do is list is on eBay and wait for bids. After the listing period is over, the person with the highest bid wins and gets to buy the product.

eBay provides a popular way for individuals to sell and buy products and services. There is an electronic platform provided where ordinary and unique items are sold. Individuals and businesses are able to purchase new and secondhand goods ranging from cars and books to clothes and holidays.

The Pros and Cons of eBay Selling

Pros

1. *Large base of shoppers:* eBay has over 171 million active users as of 2018. Having access to this huge customer base gives you an excellent chance of successfully selling your products or services.

2. *Setting up a store is very simple:* Building your own store can be a challenging affair especially if you are starting from scratch. On the other hand, setting up shop on eBay is fast, easy and convenient. Once you register with eBay, you will then get a store which you can style and personalize as you wish.

3. *Buyer and seller protection:* One of the best features of eBay is that it keeps you safe. As a seller, you are protected so that you do not lose your items or any money. Your buyers are also protected which makes eBay a secure place to do business.

4. Zero competition from eBay: eBay does not sell a single item on the platform. This means that you are not exposed to competition from the platform which could otherwise have been disastrous.

Cons

1. There are marketplace fees to pay: eBay charges sellers a fee to access the marketplace. While the fees are relatively low compared to other platforms, it is an additional cost that you have to foot.

2. Stiff competition: There are hundreds of sellers on eBay and most of them sell products that are similar to yours. This makes life a little harder as you are forced to take lower prices and this will affect your profit margins.

3. Bargain customers: While it is no longer solely an auction site, eBay has come to be known as a bargain website. There are plenty of customers or buyers who will come and bargain hard for discounts and lower prices.

4. Limited control: As a seller, you generally have very little control over what happens at your store. This is different from owning your own website. Here you are able to set the rules and have total control.

5. Occasional website changes: eBay is constantly changing its outlook in its attempt to improve the user experience. The problem is that sellers sometimes cannot adjust fast enough and this can result in losses, anger, and so on.

Which Are the Best eBay Niches?

There are numerous niches on eBay which makes finding the best selling a challenge. However, over the years, more and more customers have been going onto eBay to search for something unique to buy. They also seek new releases and similar postings.

Understanding customer purchase habits and what is trendy will enable you to sell successfully on eBay.

1. Fitness

A lot of people are into fitness. They are investing their money on fitness programs and products including dietary supplements, gym wear and accessories, smart watches and so on. The latest smartwatches are very popular, especially with exercise enthusiasts. They do not just tell time but also measure vital statistics like cholesterol levels, pulse rate, and numerous others.

2. Household security

Another popular niche on eBay is household security. There has been an increased demand for home security gadgets such as video doorbells, CCTV cameras, motion sensor cameras and so on. Many of the latest devices can be integrated with smartphones which makes it really convenient for people today.

3. Bluetooth headphones

The need for Bluetooth headphones has increased tremendously in the last couple of years. This increase was triggered by Apple Inc when they changed their policy and removed the 3.5 mm jack from their devices. Ever since that time, Bluetooth headphones have gained popularity and are selling like hot cakes.

4. Virtual reality items

Virtual reality has become really big in the last couple of days. There is growing interest in high-end devices and gadgets within this sector. Many users love the virtual reality experience and are willing to spend good money buying related products and services.

Long-Term Investing Versus Short-Term Profits

eBay provides opportunities for short-term selling and for long-term selling. This means that you can sell your items on eBay for the short term and make some money or perhaps earn a living by selling long term.

If you are business oriented and wish to earn a passive income then consider long-term selling. If you can identify a suitable product in a profitable niche, then you can sell and earn a profit in the long-term.

Selling long-term on eBay

1. Find an unbranded product that sells well. Competition is not even important at this stage.
2. Acquire sufficient volumes of the product possibly from a manufacturer in China or elsewhere around the world.
3. Create a product listing for your products and make use of GTC format. Remember to reorder the stock well in-advance as your sales increase.
4. Come up with an excellent eBay listing. Ensure that you do not just sell products but also provide the after sales service and support.

Flipping products on eBay

Flipping on eBay basically means selling some of your own products on eBay. You can also source products from other sites and sell these on eBay at a profit. The first step should be research. You need to do some research to find out which products can be successfully flipped and in what niches.

Next step, find out the cost of products on eBay. If you want to do this successfully, go and filter for "sold listings". This listing will show you sold items and the price they sold for. The next step is to open an account and set it up.

Opening an eBay account is pretty simple. Simply follow the instructions and you will be done in less than 1 minute. You can then start by flipping products lying around your house. Think about the things that you no longer have use of.

Once you have flipped things from your house, you can then start sourcing products to flip from elsewhere. There are numerous places where you can find products to flip. They include craigslist, local manufacturers, Alibaba, and so on.

You can still flip products even without having any money. Take craigslist, for instance, there are lots of free listings. Carefully examine these products and see which ones you can flip. There are others who flip cheap Amazon products on eBay for a profit. This also works even when you do not have any money. Products on Amazon and Craigslist are quite affordable while eBay buyers do not mind paying a premium.

How to Get Started on eBay

Getting started on eBay is pretty easy. You should first start by simply exploring the site. Simply visit the site and then take a look at eBay. There are several informative pages available. Read the information provided on these pages and see what it says.

eBay is an online auction website. Sellers have accounts where they sell products while buyers visit eBay to buy products. If you are a buyer, then you can browse through the categories such as video games, computers, clothing and accessories, boats, and antiques.

As you browse the different titles, you might come across something that you like. When you do, then you should place a bid on it. Look at the details on the item and decide that you really want to buy.

You can place a bid on an item that you like. When you do, then you should understand that you are entering into a contractual agreement. The agreement requires you to buy the item if you win the auction. However, the seller is not obligated to sell if bidders do not get to the reserve price.

Sometimes you may not want to bid on an item but buy it directly. You will see a tab marked, "Buy Now". Click on this tab in order to buy the product at the indicated price and not the bid price. There are numerous ways of paying on eBay, including the use of electronic payments, personal check, cash, and cashier's checks. Registering on eBay is free so register first and then sell or buy whatever it is that you want.

Selling on eBay

When you start to sell your products on eBay, you may just have begun your successful online business. Selling on eBay is fast and easy. You can start slowly by a side project and then grow it into a fully fledged business.

Open an account: The first step is to open an account with eBay. eBay can actually provide you with a name if you like but you are free to choose your own. Once you have a name that is approved by eBay you should then open an account.

The process of opening an eBay account is also pretty straightforward. First, visit eBay's homepage and find the "Log in" link. This is where the registration process begins. Provide your name, an email address, and other details. eBay will confirm your email account after which your account will be confirmed.

Payment method: Once the account is set up, you should choose a payment method. There are numerous payment methods available, so provide as many of them as you possibly can. Some of the most popular payment options available include the use of PayPal as well as credit cards such as Visa and MasterCard.

Reputation: Now that you are all set up and your account is up and running, you should build your reputation by purchasing a few items. When you buy some items, you will get some positive feedback in that you are an honest and diligent customer. This will give you sufficient boost in reputation to start selling.

Set up your profile page so people may have a basic idea about who you are. You do not need to have a very elaborate profile so a basic one will do. However, if you plan on selling very expensive items, then you should probably add a little more information other than the basics.

Choose what to sell: By this stage, you should know what you are going to sell. If you do not then you should pause and think about it. Consider selling items that you are familiar with. You should also learn which items are prohibited and cannot be sold on the platform. To minimize risk at the onset, you should focus on selling only items that you have.

There are shipping and logistics matters that you need to consider. When you sell something on eBay and someone buys it, you will have to ship it out to them. This can be a costly affair so think about logistics, shipping, and storage.

Potential Investment

If you want to start selling on eBay, then you will need a budget. This budget can be as low as $100 or as high as $5,000 depending on various factors. Some of these factors include the items that you intend to sell, the account you choose on eBay, shipping costs, and the size and cost of merchandise.

If you are a beginner, then you probably will not need a lot more than $1,000. This amount will cover your eBay costs, shipping costs, cost of merchandise, storage and other administrative costs and overheads.

Try and keep your costs as low as possible. You can do this by avoiding all unnecessary costs and expenses.

Also, identify a storage facility where your products will be stored. If you are buying products in bulk then you may want to pay for storage. However, you can always store any merchandise at home. Finally, think about the cost of shipping. Your customers could be from anywhere in America from the East Coast all the way to the West Coast. Find affordable yet reliable shipping solutions so that you become profitable and thrive.

Mistakes Often Made by eBay Sellers

1. High shipping fees: One of the biggest mistakes people make is to pay hefty shipping fees to have items shipped to buyers.

2. A Lack of text on images: A lot of the time sellers will provide images but then forget to provide descriptive text. Such text is crucial as it lets potential buyers know about the products.

3. Poor quality images: Sometimes it is worse to use a bad photo than not use one at all. Always ensure that you take good quality photos and only post the best photos that are clear and colorful.

4. Only thinking locally: Too many sellers only think locally yet they stand to make so much more money by selling internationally. Always think about attracting more buyers to your products.

5. Getting the price wrong: As a seller, you can either lose money or lose potential customers if you do not price your products correctly. If your price is too high, then you will send away customers. Low prices mean you are losing profits.

Chapter 6: Facebook Advertising

Introduction to Facebook Advertising

It is almost impossible to browse through Facebook without coming across an advertisement. These are often targeting messages and it is why we are always tempted to click through and find out more. Facebook advertisements provide the best opportunity for reaching a targeted yet wide audience on a budget. Such adverts can be done at a very cost-effective price.

A powerful tool to get your product or service out there

The best part about Facebook advertising is that you can create ads that are targeted towards a particular demographic. The ads are not just affordable but very cost effective. Here is a look at what is actually involved in Facebook advertising.

Here is the process of creating an audience for your Facebook ads

First, create a list of between 15 and 20 influencers in your chosen niche. The influencers could be organizations, influential individuals with a huge following, publications, and so on.

Enter the influencers into the interest box one at a time. Some will be indexed but others will not. Just click on the ones that are indexed. Once this is done, go and click on Page Likes. Facebook will display a wide variety of pages and the affinity score of each.

To increase your audience's affinity, delete and add interests. If you are happy with your audience, press the Create Ad button and Facebook will do so automatically. All the new audience will be transferred to your advertisement. It is advisable to save your audience just in case you want to use the same targeted audience again.

Facebook Ads

Facebook provides you with two different tools to create and manage ads. There is the Power Editor and the Ads Manager. The Power Editor is great for those who run and manage plenty of ads while the Ads Manager is a tool that is suitable for anyone seeking to place Facebook ads.

The best aspect of Facebook is that you do not need to be a professional marketer or an advertising expert. Facebook is designed such that anyone can place an ad. This advertising tool levels the playing for individuals and businesses, both small and large. If you take your time, you will learn how to create low cost yet effective ads for your business.

How to Create Facebook Ads

If you are a marketer or just an ordinary person looking to place an advertisement on Facebook, then you will have a couple of options to choose from. The options are actually three and they are;

1. *Campaigns:* campaigns consist of all assets that belong to you

2. *Ad sets:* These allow you to target separate audiences with different characteristics because you will need individual ads for each audience

3. *Ordinary ads:* The ads that you create exist within ad sets. Ad sets can contain a variety of advertisements which vary in terms of images, color, and so on

Determine your preferred editor

Facebook makes use of two different tools when it comes to creating paid ads. These tools are the Power Editor and the Ads Manager. In order to determine which of the two is most suitable, consider factors such as the number of ads you wish to post, the size of your company, and so on.

Most individuals and small businesses fare well with Ads Manager. However, for large companies and those placing numerous advertisements, they are best served by the Power Editor. The Power Editor is best suited for larger advertisers who prefer to take charge over their campaigns.

Select your objective

The Ad Manager on Facebook is designed to best handle your campaigns. Therefore, before starting your campaign, you will be required to select an objective. You have about 10 different objectives to choose from such as directing traffic to your website and so on.

Identify your audience

Now you need to determine who your audience is. You will probably need to experiment with a couple of targeting options so that you eventually identify the audience that you want. Facebook has made targeting an audience really simple. For instance, if you are searching to create brand awareness, then you should opt for a more general audience. Facebook gives you options to target your audience, such as age, gender, language, location, and many others.

Set your budget

As an advertiser, you will need to set your budget. There are two main options for setting your budget. These are a lifetime budget and daily budget. The daily budget allows you to set an ad and run it through the day. The minimum amount for this budget is $1. The lifetime budget allows you to select your budget for a set period of time.

Create your advertisement

At this stage, you will now create your ad. It will be up to you to determine what it looks like. Fortunately, Facebook will offer you options that will make your work easier. There are carousels and links provided if you are looking to send traffic to your website. Once ready, you can begin running your ads. As they run, keep monitoring just to know how well they are performing.

Kind of Results to Expect

Facebook advertising is a very effective tool. You will reach your targeted audience because Facebook makes it possible to choose which demographic views your ads.

The results you expect to receive will vary depending on certain factors. These include country where the advertisement is targeted, nichc, and also the type of advertisement. The one thing you can be happy with is that Facebook is one of the most effective advertising and marketing platforms on the internet.

According to a case study on Facebook advertising, you can expect to receive an average ROI of 450%. This means that for every $1 you invest in Facebook advertising, you can expect to earn at least $450. Gravity Defyer is a shoe retailer who used Facebook advertising and received this ROI. Others have seen an even better return. It all depends on the factors described above.

Facebook Advertising Secrets You May Not Be Aware Of

There are certain secrets that you may not be aware of. One of these is "Audience Insights". This is a feature provided by Facebook that shows you the latest trends about your current and potential customers. By simply collecting emails, you get to learn about the buying activity, page likes, Facebook usage and so much more about your email list members.

You can use Facebook's latest feature to help you retarget your current or existing customers. This feature is known as

Facebook's custom audience and will show you the visitors that landed on your website via your Facebook advertisement. We also have Ads Reporting which is a feature that reveals more detailed information to you.

Chapter 7: Getting Traffic

It is crucial as an online seller and business owner to drive traffic to your website or platform where your products or services are found. The traffic consists of general web visitors, your readers, followers, sales leads, potential and existing customers.

Web traffic is important because of a number of reasons. It is a pointer to how effective your marketing campaigns are working, provides insights about your audience, improves search engine credibility and will bring in more customers. By working hard and applying some inbound marketing techniques, you can attract more traffic to your website. There are different ways of achieving this. We will examine two or three different effective ways of getting traffic.

Social Media Marketing

The term social media marketing refers to a type of internet marketing technique that makes use of social networking sites. These sites are used as a marketing tool. The aim of social media marketing is to develop content that users will then share with others on their social media pages.

For a successful social media marketing campaign, you will need to do some optimization. SMO or social media optimization is the process of optimizing content in order to attract new and unique visitors to your website. There are two main ways of conducting SMO. One is to promote certain activities through social media such as updating tweets, statuses, or blog posts. The other is to add sharing buttons and RSS feeds and other sharing buttons to social media content.

Social media marketing enables firms to obtain direct feedback from consumers and potential customers. This helps to make the firm appear more relatable. Social media interactions allow customers the opportunity to air complaints and ask questions thereby getting the feeling that their opinions count. Experts refer to this kind of activity as social customer relationship management or social CRM.

Social media websites like Facebook, LinkedIn, Instagram, and Twitter have made social media marketing even more common. Due to the growing interest of this marketing process, the government, through the Federal Trade Commission, has stepped in to introduce minor regulations. These are meant to protect consumers and other participants such as bloggers from exploitation.

Social Media Advertising

Social media advertising is part of digital advertising. This particular type of advertising focuses on placing advertising messages on social media websites. The five largest social media sites at the moment include Facebook, Twitter, LinkedIn, Pinterest and Google+. Others include YouTube, MySpace, Instagram, and so on. These sites are very attractive to advertisers and the main reason is that of their vast reach. Placing a targeted advertisement on one of these websites can have a huge impact as the ad is likely to reach tens of millions of possible customers.

While these social media sites have vast numbers of followers, the best part is that the huge audience can be segmented. When segmented to the micro level, it becomes easier for advertisers to target particular demographics. Companies find social media websites with over 10 million followers quite attractive. This is because even when segmented, the numbers are still attractive.

Think about a company that is selling gardening equipment. A social network with over 1 billion users may have over 10 million gardening enthusiasts. These can be further subdivided into flower garden lovers, landscaping enthusiasts and so on. Such demographics are extremely attractive to advertisers. One of the best demographics available is geographic. You are able to geographically target consumers not just at country level but down to state, zip, and even city.

Different social media

Generally, not all social media websites are suitable for all advertisements. Some of more suitable, in some instance, more than others. Also, these social media networks offer varying advertising options. As such, not all are suitable for all purposes.

Therefore, when considering a social network to place your advertisement, consider the ones that are naturally performing well. Think about social networking sites where your content performs well and is generally well accepted by your audience.

Different social networks have different demographics. For instance, Pinterest has more female than users while Snapchat has much younger users compared to other networks.

Why Is Social Media Advertising Necessary?

Generating leads: One of the reasons why anyone would consider social media advertising is to generate leads. Each advertisement posted should have a link to a landing page. Your landing pages should have a call to action.

Contact an engaged audience: Most social media users are often highly engaged in one topic or other. The reason is that most users visit social media to engage others on certain issues. It is easy to interact and engage with such an audience.

To increase visibility: When you advertise your company, products, or brand on social media, you also get to increase your visibility. More and more consumers will get to view your company and brand and hence become aware of the amazing products you are selling.

Increase customer loyalty and brand awareness: Advertising has the added advantage of increasing brand awareness. Users on platforms such as Facebook and Instagram will visit your page and like it hence increase popularity. A social media page provides you the opportunity to interact with your customers and followers and this ensures your business is at the top of their minds all the time.

Target a particular audience: Advertising through social media enables you to target a demographic that you desire. The reason is that social media users tend to reveal plenty of personal information. This information can be collected, analyzed, and thereafter processed so that it is categorized in a manner that is of use to marketers and advertisers.

Social media advertising enables marketers or business owners to place targeted adverts in a cost-effective manner. This kind of approach has been extremely successful because of the relatively low cost as well as the effectiveness of the adverts.

The ultimate goal of any advertising campaign is to bring in new clients and ultimately more revenue. It is therefore important for a business owner or an entrepreneur to determine how to use social media advertising and which particular social media to choose.

1. Advertising on LinkedIn

LinkedIn is a popular social networking site often used by professionals, company executives and others in the corporate world. Therefore, the advertisements and marketing messages placed on this social network should be geared towards this demographic.

You can launch targeted adverts within minutes by using the self-service solutions provided. The benefit of using LinkedIn is that it lets you set your own budget, opt for impressions or clicks, and then stop the advertisement at any time. There is a Campaign Manager provided to help you with all these steps.

The Campaign Manager is a tool that enables you to post different kinds of campaigns. These include Text Ads, Sponsored In-Mail, and Sponsored Content. You also have another choice known as Dynamic Ads. These allow you to join efforts with a marketing team at LinkedIn in order to produce highly visible and exclusively placed ads targeted at a premium audience.

Placing adverts on LinkedIn is a pretty simple process. The first step is to open an account if you do not already have one. Start by signing in to the Campaign Manager as the entire process will occur here.

Once you are ready, you will then choose your preferred advertisement format. There are a couple of formats including Text Ads, Sponsored In-Mail, Sponsored Content or just a mixture of these formats. Then provide the content of the ads including any video, photos, and text. As soon as you are ready, you should then create the ads.

When the ads are ready, you can decide to target a particular audience. This is a simple process so once done, you simply post your ad and let your audience view it.

2. Advertising on Instagram

Advertising on Instagram is very similar to Facebook advertising. This should not come as a big surprise because Facebook owns Instagram. On both platforms, there is no set price so you get to choose how much to spend.

There are different ways of advertising and telling your story on Instagram. You can post video ads, carousel ads, photo ads, and stories ads. Buying ads is easy because you have various options. You can purchase ads within the app, via the ads manager or through Instagram partners.

The costs are pretty low and affordable. As an advertiser, you should expect to pay anywhere between $0.2 and $2 per click for

CPC advertising. On the other hand, you can choose the cost per mille or CPM advertising which costs about $5 per 1000 visitors. Instagram is more effective than Facebook because the CTR or click-through rate is 0.8% compared to Facebook's 0.6%.

3. YouTube Advertising

Another great way of attracting customers is to place ads on YouTube. However, YouTube advertisements are very different from those on other social media. You need certain knowledge in order to place any YouTube ads. Fortunately, you will get plenty of options as well.

There are generally three types of YouTube video ads. These include the True View ads, Pre-roll and Bumper ads. The most common are True View ads. As an advertiser, you only get to pay when viewers or users actually interact with or watch the video ads. The videos are pretty simple to customize which makes sharing quite easy.

You will only be required to pay if viewers watch at least 30 seconds of the video or if they click on a call to action at the end of the advert. The other type is the Video Discovery. These ads show up on YouTube's results page, homepage, and in related YouTube videos. Basically, these are YouTube videos that appeared following a search.

We then have the In-stream ads. True View In-Stream ads are the ones that play just before a video begins. These provide viewers with an option to skip them after about 5 to 10 seconds. Marketers are able to customize their ads using different CTAs as well as overlay texts.

Pre-roll ads are almost forced ads because viewers do not have the option of skipping. However, they can be played before, midway, or after the main video. These ads are usually between 15 and 20 seconds long.

Creating and setting up ads on YouTube is equally easy. However, you may need some assistance preparing the actual ad video. Fortunately, there are plenty of video editing apps in the market that can help you prepare your own YouTube ads. As usual, you will need to have a YouTube or Gmail account and a payment system such as PayPal.

Chapter 8: Getting a VA to Create a Highly Passive Business

There is a misconception out there, that virtual assistants are expensive and a luxury. Some think that only big businesses can afford them. However, this is not necessarily the case because numerous small businesses and freelancers actually work with virtual assistants.

What is a virtual assistant? A virtual assistant is basically a remote professional that provides assistance to businesses and individuals. They often handle online tasks. A virtual assistant can be located anywhere in the world and can take on multiple clients. You can hire a virtual assistant to assist you to accomplish a variety of tasks on a daily or regular basis.

You may have to train your virtual assistant over a Skype call to run the business how you want, or maybe the Assistant is already skilled in what you need them to do.

Many small business owners resort to hiring virtual assistants because of the limited time they have. A virtual assistant provides a solution to this problem. Most small business owners realize that, while their businesses are promising and also doing well, there is a lot of work that cannot be done by one person. Having a dedicated person providing the necessary assistance can help your business thrive and take it to the next level.

Hiring a virtual assistant to the point where the business becomes stable and passive is more of a necessity rather than a luxury. A hired virtual assistant is also likely to do a much better job compared to a physical assistant. A physical assistant takes more time and effort to manage compared to a virtual one.

What Can A Virtual Assistant Help Me With?

The real answer here is anything, just train them up and you can pay them for their time and work.

Specifically, VA's can help you with:

Customer service tasks: These include answering phone calls and sending emails

Store management: Tasks here include sales management, inventory management, and order fulfillment

Data entry: A virtual assistant can help with bookkeeping and data input from various sources and onto a spreadsheet

Cold calling: Making calls using a script and scheduling meetings

Research: They can perform research on your behalf to find specific information that is crucial for your business. For instance, they can search for influencers

Personal errands: A virtual assistant can help you accomplish certain tasks such as getting flowers delivered and so on

Social media management: Assistants help by responding to comments, curating content and all other similar tasks

Graphic Design: If you constantly need designs, you can outsource this easily to a VA.

Benefits of Having A Virtual Assistant

A virtual assistance is a lot more affordable than a physical or in-house assistant. The physical assistant costs more yet they need frequent training. You also have to pay additional costs such as insurance. You will need one whose personality matches yours if you are to spend a lot of time together.

Your small business needs assistance but can hardly afford to pay a full-time employee. The assistance that you need can easily be provided by a virtual assistant at affordable rates. This gives you a chance to do other things as your business grows but without paying a premium for it.

A virtual assistant saves you the cost and effort of holding interviews. Interviews may reveal individuals searching for a job but not necessarily experienced assistants.

Things to consider when hiring a virtual assistant

If you are grappling with some of the challenges that new businesses undergo, then you should seriously consider hiring a virtual assistant. However, you need to hire an experienced virtual assistant who understands what needs to be done and can help you get the job done efficiently.

There are plenty of duties and jobs that you can outsource to a virtual assistant. These include human resource management, accounting jobs, or simple administrative tasks. However, the first question that you should ask is what do I need a virtual assistant for? Think about all the tedious, repetitive tasks around your business. What do you need help with the most? Is it responding to clients' emails? Posting on social media?

You should prioritize your tasks and find out which ones you can do and which ones you need help with. Some business owners simply need an assistant with whom they can work closely together. Other assistants are able to provide personal services such as book appointments, handle schedules, and micro-tasks.

When it comes to virtual assistants, we generally have two options. We have individual virtual assistants and then companies that provide the assistants. An individual assistant is best when you feel the need to work with someone closely to accomplish tasks. A company works much better when you have specific tasks that you want to be done.

Where to Find A Virtual Assistant

1. Online Job Platforms

Some of the best places to find jobs include online job platforms. These include websites such as Upwork, Guru, and Fivver. These platforms have review systems that ensure quality and keep virtual assistants accountable.

2. VA Networking

There are professional VA networking websites that you can contact. These networks have forums and platforms where they exchange ideas, discuss matters, and assist employers to find trustworthy virtual assistants.

2. Industry related seminars, workshops, and gatherings

When you attend events such as seminars and workshops, try and consult your network about VA recommendations.

3. Various VA websites

There are plenty of VA websites out there. They include Zirtual, www.zirtual.com, and VANetworking at www.vanetworking.com. Check these sites out for experienced and vetted VAs.

Personally my favorite site is Fiverr. If you are going to try and take business with them that's more than the job you need from Fiverr, or you need them to privately run a task within your business, then DO NOT ask them through the Fiverr messenger. Instead, create the message on a word document and then screenshot that message, sending that to them on Fiverr. This is loophole around Fiverr finding out that you are taking business from them and going private.

9/10 VA's will give you their Facebook, if they trust you and see more work for them!

The truth about Fast Tracking Your Success

Take a Course to Enhance your Business Skills

If you want to grow your business, understand the various aspects, and thrive, then you should consider learning a business course. You do not need to go to business school and spend years taking a degree or diploma course. There are plenty of successful entrepreneurs who never did.

You probably do not have the money to hire professionals and even if you hire virtual assistants, it is crucial that you understand all the different aspects of your business from social media marketing to bookkeeping, inventory management, taxes and so on.

Essential skills to start and build an online business

As an entrepreneur seeking to start and manage your online business, it is crucial that you acquire certain important skills. These skills will help you build your business and ensure that it is both thriving and long-term profitable.

As a business owner, there are things that you need to learn. For instance, you need to learn how to reach out to customers, how to select the right kind of products and services as well as the right kind of marketing tactics and strategies. Here are some crucial skills you can learn that will enhance your business.

1. Social media marketing: Hundreds of millions of individuals, including potential customers, get onto different social media sites to interact, socialize and share with others.

2. Bookkeeping: You need to learn the basics of bookkeeping. This is a crucial course that will help you manage your finance and determine how profitable your business is. Bookkeeping will help you understand crucial financial statements including income statement, cash flow statements, balance sheet, and so on.

3. *Customer service:* You will learn how to handle customers, how to address their needs, phone etiquette, and how to keep things positive at all times.

4. *Inbound digital marketing course:* Digital marketing will expose you to the world of internet marketing techniques that will attract quality leads and potential customers to your website.

Where to Study These Courses

1. Short courses at Google Digital Workshop

Google offers entrepreneurs free short courses to enhance their skills. The comprehensive program covers topics such as building a web presence, email marketing, digital marketing, mobile marketing, and search engine marketing. These courses are offered to beginners and are completely free.

2. Free courses at Alison.com

If you are a busy individual but still need to learn some skills, then another great place to take a course is Alison.com. This is a platform that offers plenty of free short courses which can be studied remotely and concluded within a few weeks' time.

3. Courses at Udemy

One place to learn a course is at Udemy. Visit Udemy at www.udemy.com. Udemy is a leading online learning platform that teaches courses using a different approach than the ordinary classroom. You can find numerous practical courses available on this platform. There are also plenty of different business courses that will help to inform you and educate on you on all matters pertaining to business. These are usually cheaper courses that don't go into to immense detail so make sure you do your research and find realistic and honest testimonials.

4. Constant Contact

One of the most reputable platforms where you can learn all about online marketing courses is at Constant Contact. Www.constantcontact.com is a great platform to learn all about digital marketing on Pinterest, YouTube, Facebook, and even blogging.

5. YouTube Courses

This is what I recommend. You can find plenty of other courses on YouTube. A lot of experienced business owners and trainers have designed video courses which are fun, easy to follow, and easy to understand. You can search for business courses that are suitable for you on YouTube so that you acquire the crucial skills that you need.

If you are going to buy a course off of someone from YouTube or Instagram, make sure they have been in the field for over a year. You have to be careful of people selling courses that have just had quick success and don't really know what they're talking about. Find someone you can trust, with experience and people you can reach out to for help.

Bonus 50 Passive Income Ideas

These are other Ideas that you can dive into that 100% make money online today! The importance of having an open mind is key.

<u>50 other passive Income Ideas could be:</u>

1) Blogging
2) Niche Site
3) eBay Selling
4) Personal Brand
5) Amazon FBA
6) Cryptocurrency Investing
7) Self-publishing
8) Network Marketing
9) Real estate investing REITS
10) Index Funds

11) Build a software
12) Manage a social media consulting company
13) Air BNB
14) Create an Online Course
15) Youtuber
16) ATM Business
17) Create An app
18) Rent what you own Clothing,
19) Rent your own Car 23) Rent your space (for people to work)
20) Create T-shirts (Merch by Amazon)

21) Stock Market Investing
22) Sell Stock Photos
23) Create a Camparosin site
24) Games Machine Business
25) Laundromat business
26) Buy an existing online business one that you know you will

profit from)
27) Retail Arbitrage
28) Build an Instagram Page
29) Build a Facebook Page
30) Create A podcast

31) Buy domain Names and Park them (a bit dodgy)
32) Get Cashback rewards on credit cards
33) Free Lancing
34) Promote events through a freelancer on your account
35) Car Flipping
36) Online Surveys
37) Storage facility
38) Buy a Do it yourself car wash facility
39) Buy a Do it yourself dog wash facility
40) Design products and sell on rebubble or cafepress

41) Peer to peer investing
42) SEO consulting
43) Facebook Advertising Consultant
44) Starting a subscription based company (Eg. Spotify, Netflix)
45) Downloading apps that make you quick passive income
46) Invest with robo advisor
47) House sitting (Free rent and can also get paid)
48) Advertise on your car
49) Vending Machine Business
50) Phone Flipping

Looking in to these, ideas you'll be shocked at how easy it is to create passive income through them. Enjoy the journey, be patient, but HUSTLE hard.

Conclusion

The next step is to identify the right kind of online business that is suitable for you. There are numerous businesses out there so you need to identify the one that you have a passion for and one that is going to thrive and succeed in the long term. Having passion, knowledge, and experience in a particular business will give you a head start in the specific business that you choose.

You do not need to worry if you have a job or other occupation because most business owners work other jobs on a full-time basis. The thing is that you can always find time to work on your online business. Starting such a business is not difficult and is not costly. However, you will need to put in some time and hard work so that your business succeeds eventually.

If you adopt a good business and marketing strategy, work hard, and take your customers' concerns seriously, then you will be able to establish a successful business that will provide you with a passive income for many years to come. You can also grow and expand your business such that you may not need to work a nine-to-five job anymore. There are numerous successful online business owners out there and you can become one of them too.

Finally, if you found this book useful in any way, a review on Amazon is always appreciated!